REBELS IN PARADISE

The Inside Story of the Battle for Celtic Football Club

David Low and Francis Shennan

MAINSTREAM
PUBLISHING

EDINBURGH AND LONDON

First published in Great Britain in 1994 by
MAINSTREAM PUBLISHING COMPANY (EDINBURGH) LTD
7 Albany Street
Edinburgh EH1 3UG

ISBN 1 85158 677 6

A catalogue record for this book is available from the British
Library

Typeset in Palatino by Litho Link Limited, Welshpool, Powys

Printed in Great Britain by Butler & Tanner Ltd, Frome

CONTENTS

We dedicate this book, with love, to . . .

Noelle and our children   my parents
Christian, Patrick and   Tom and Cecilia
        Joshua Low   Shennan

. . . and we offer our thanks, with gratitude, to

everybody who helped Celtic Football Club achieve change
and who helped with the preparation of this book. It is part
of the unwritten culure of football that a man, or woman, is
judged by the deeds he performs and the sense, or
otherwise, that he speaks, rather than by his money and
status. That is especially true of a club like Celtic.

In that spirit we list those we wish to thank individually
in simple alphabetical order. As so many people did so
much, it is possible someone will be overlooked. Our
apologies if that is the case; you know the contribution you
made and we thank you for it. Our special thanks to:

Celts For Change, Jo Clark, David Cunningham, Brian
Dempsey, Betty Devlin, Jim Doherty, Hugh Drake, Colin
Duncan, Jack Flanagan, Bill Gallacher, Tommy Gallacher,
Glens of Antrim Celtic Supporters Club, Willie 'T.C.'
Haughey, Dominic Keane, Edmund Keane, John Keane,
Mark Keane, Fergus McCann, Kevin McCarra, Michael
McDonald, Kevin McKenna, Matt McGlone, Gerry McNee,
Paul McNeill, Oliver Magill, Peter Maley, Len Murray,
Aiden Neeson, Brendan Sweeney, John 'Double Agent'
Thompson, David Watt, Gerald Weisfeld . . . and, in the end,
Jimmy Farrell, Tom Grant, Kevin Kelly and Jack McGinn.

INTRODUCTION

GOOD FRIDAY fell on 1 April in 1994, but to supporters of the 'grand old team' it had already fallen on 4 March. That was the name they gave to the day when the deal once thought impossible was done. The so-called rebels walked into the football ground the fans knew as 'Paradise' to end a 106-year dynasty and take control of Celtic Football Club.

It marked the end of a carefully planned campaign which became one of the most public stories of the 1990s, or so it appeared. Every possible angle of the story seemed to be covered in the papers and on radio and television, not just in Scotland but throughout Britain, in Ireland and in Canada. But beneath the avalanche of headlines the real story remained hidden.

The sheer scale of the media coverage actually helped to obscure the truth. When, on 19 January 1992, the story first broke that a group of businessmen were putting together an attempt to take control of Celtic, vast numbers of people said it could never happen. The story was denied the same day in another Sunday newspaper. One of the two journalists who broke the story was Francis Shennan. The man denying the story was David Low. It was a sign of how sensitive the situation was that Low felt obliged to deny it, and it remained sensitive in varying degrees for the next two years. The media could only report the story as it unfolded, and distractions and diversions were constantly appearing. Names were mentioned which had no part in the story – or only a walk-on part. Public pronouncements were made while deals were done behind closed doors.

One man was at every crucial meeting in the battle to rescue Celtic Football Club. David Low conceived the method for the takeover plan, briefed first Brian Dempsey, then Fergus McCann, and all of the many people who were essential in making the plan work, from the millionaire investors to modest but loyal shareholders. He travelled Britain, Ireland and North America, signing up shareholders' support or buying their shares. If there was a deal to be done, he would go there, whether to an international hotel or a cow shed. When the rebels fell out, he acted as go-between so they could unite again. When the two halves of the rebel coalition competed to complete a takeover deal, he pushed through the one which was successful. His signature is on the document that rescued the club from receivership with just eight minutes to spare.

This is the inside story of the battle for Celtic Football Club, based on exclusive access to transcripts and diaries. It is not the historical overview, nor is it a business book. From the start we decided against having a dozen voices giving their accounts, re-interpreting their behaviour with the benefit of hindsight. We wanted to convey the excitement, the tension, the pressure of the story as it unfolded. It is written in the third person, like a thriller, and events moved at that kind of pace. Because we take you so close to the story, we concentrate on the central events of the last four years. There is enough to take in without re-hashing material already well covered in the papers. Similarly we mention, but do go into the details of, earlier attempts at change.

In 1988 Fergus McCann tried to help Celtic Football Club to expand, to move into the modern era and give the club a stadium to match so that they could become a viable business. Long before the Taylor Report and Celtic's financial crises, he proposed increasing the seating capacity from 9,000 to 24,000, providing standing accommodation for 48,000 and offered a low-interest loan and marketing help to bring it about. This was the first of a number of ideas. He was ready to make an offer to all the shareholders but the board made it clear they would oppose him. The man whose money and determination saved Celtic from receivership was treated as a threat. Yet as he told shareholders in November 1993:

> We are not enemies of Celtic. We are entitled to be as big supporters of Celtic as anyone. The fact that we are not members of two families should not disqualify us from financing and helping to invest in Celtic Football Club . . . The club was never intended to be a family business. It was started to improve the lot of poor families in the east end of Glasgow. It developed into an institution with which thousands of people feel they have a family connection . . . more than that, they feel it is part of their identity . . .
>
> On the field, as everybody knows, no success is guaranteed because of money only. However, I can guarantee you one thing: in professional team sports at the level Celtic are expected to play at, with no money you are guaranteed no success. We, the shareholders, have a responsibility to the supporters, who pay their money every week, to deliver success. In fact, more than shareholders, we too are Celtic supporters.

Because we take you so close to the story, we show you the differences which emerged between allies. There were disagreements about the best tactics, the most direct route to their goal, how to achieve the fairest outcome for supporters and shareholders. We open with the race between the McCann and Weisfeld teams to clinch a deal, but they were really on the same side. It was not a clash of factions, but two flanks of the same army anxious to seize the same objective. If the communications between the two flanks had been better, they might have saved themselves time and money.

There might be heroes in this story but no saints. There are certainly strong personalities: men who have become millionaires by their own efforts, used to having their own way. The surprise is not that there were disagreements but that there were not more. Yet they were able to submerge those differences for the sake of a near-bankrupt little company in the east end of Glasgow. In part that explains why this is not a business book. The underlying financial position is central to the story but there is no need to be able to read the business pages to understand it. Business was the pitch on which the game was played, it was not the game itself. The game was the struggle to save the soul of an institution that was almost more of an ideal than a football club.

Rebels in Paradise tells the story of the Celtic takeover as it has never been told before. It reveals the plan and the purpose behind the often confusing surface events. It explains why future events will unfold as they do, and it will give you an insight into the hidden world of the football business. But, more importantly, it will give you an insight into what men – rich and poor alike – will do in pursuit of their ideal.

David Low and Francis Shennan,
Glasgow, May 1994

Chapter One

REBELS AT THE GATES

A manager needs serious money to operate in today's transfer market and I have a major job on to get the players Celtic require to be a major force once again.
    – Lou Macari, talking to Hugh Keevins of *The Scotsman*

ON SATURDAY, 12 February 1994, Celtic looked like a team that revelled in producing last-minute results. They had not won for two months, and had not won away from home for four – in fact, not since the first match with Lou Macari as manager back in October. But Macari's new signing from Sheffield United, Willie Falconer, and Charlie Nicholas kept pressing forward and two minutes before half-time Nicholas took advantage of an error by Hearts' goalkeeper, Henry Smith, to smash the ball home. In the second half they waited until seven minutes from time before Pat McGinlay charged into Hearts' penalty area then laid the ball back for Nicholas to shoot sweet and low.

Next day, however, the biggest headline was 'Paradise Lost', as the *Sunday Mail*, one of the Mirros Group's two Scottish tabloids, predicted the board were about to sell out to a group of Glasgow businessmen, Willie Haughey, Gerald Weisfeld and Paul Waterson. The story might well have come true had not another group been more prepared.

13

Two days before the game three men met in the well-lit and tastefully furnished offices of the accountancy firm, Pannell Kerr Forster. The offices were in a restored Victorian terrace in Carlton Place, overlooking the pedestrian suspension bridge that crosses the Clyde in the heart of Glasgow. This solid backdrop had once doubled for Moscow in the television fild about traitor Guy Burgess, *An Englishman Abroad.*

The meeting was held to discuss the impending collapse of a century-old dynasty which had led the potentially richest football club in Britain to the brink of bankruptcy. The club had fanatical support throughout Britain and Ireland and even in Canada and the United States. It had an unparalleled history of success, taking its place in the forefront of Scottish soccer from its first year, and was the first British club to win a European trophy. It was harder to remember that it had been an innovator off the field too, building and maintaining one of the best grounds in Scotland while incurring hardly any debt.

The collapse of that dynasty would mark the end of a two-year campaign to achieve what everyone had once thought impossible, the takeover of a club where three families could block anyone they disliked from buying shares: two years of secret meetings and clandestine deals in bizarre locations, from luxury apartments in Montreal, Arizona and the Caribbean to a Belfast graveyard and a Fermanagh cowshed.

But that meeting also marked the start of a three-week nail-biting climax in which three millionaires separated by continents would wrestle to seize an opportunity that would never come again. For three weeks in 1994, control of Celtic Football Club was up for grabs and the fight would go to the limit, settled with only eight minutes to spare.

The three men at the meeting were advisors to the Celtic Investor Group, but the supporters already knew the Group as 'the rebels', or the alliance of Scots-Canadian millionaire Fergus McCann and Glasgow building boss Brian Dempsey. The fans might have recognised one of the men there, but not Charles Barnett of Pannell Kerr Forster, and Robert Bain, managing director of the public relations company, Charles Barker Scotland Ltd. They were, respectively, McCann's financial and PR advisers in Scotland.

Only the face of the third, corporate adviser, David Low, might have been familiar from newspaper stories or brief television appearances. For, two years and four months before, he had taken a plan for the takeover of Celtic to Brian Dempsey.

Low had already held one of his regular morning meetings with Dempsey. At lunchtime he had met Willie Haughey and now he briefed McCann's advisers. Haughey's plan was to buy the 12,000 shares held by the Celtic board and their families at £300 a share. The £3.6 million cost of this would be split between Haughey, hotel and pub owner Paul Waterson, Gerald Weisfeld, millionaire and former owner of the What Everyone Wants chain, and his stepson Michael McDonald. The idea, said Low, was naive and contained no real plans for Celtic's future even if they did buy control.

Celtic were facing a large outflow of cash in the remaining five months of the financial year. There were only seven home games left in the season, all against teams with a poor track record of support. They had still to pay the £350,000 which Macari had agreed for Falconer and would face a substantial bill for Lee Martin. They had offered £150,000 against Manchester United's asking price of £500,000 and both clubs had agreed to let an independent transfer tribunal decide. (A month after the win over Hearts the tribunal set the price at £350,000.)

Charlie Nicholas was believed to be owed £100,000 from the time he re-signed for the club. Former chief executive Terry Cassidy was suing the club over his dismissal for £143,000 and the legal expenses, if they lost, could take the cost over £200,000. The number of Executive Club members had fallen and former members were asking for the money they were owed by the club. Season tickey income for 1994-95 was expected to be poor. Money still had to be spent on Parkhead to increase the seating capacity and £431,000 had already been paid to consultants for work on the Cambuslang stadium plan.

It was a long and sorry list. Celtic's only hope for the future was for control to pass out of the dynasty of three families which had dominated it into the hands of a new generation of professional businessmen. The advisors' view

15

was that McCann and Dempsey must act on the latest developments or risk being frozen out of Celtic's future. The question was: How?

Three months earlier, on 26 November 1993, the two men, and their team of friends, supporters and advisors had requisitioned an extraordinary general meeting of shareholders to call for a fresh issue of shares to inject £13.8 million into the cash-starved club. On a show of hands, the vote had been tied at 47 each but if it had gone to a count of shares rather than shareholders they would have been defeated by the combined voting power of five directors. Besides, they needed a two-thirds majority to have new shares issued. With that defeat, McCann and Dempsey had publicly declared they were withdrawing their offer. What they really did was to withdraw out of sight, like a besieging army withdrawing behind a hill, waiting for the moment they knew must eventually come.

The advisors decided to carry out a search at Companies House to examine the accounts of Haughey's company, City Refrigeration. It was common practice to find out as much as possible about their rivals. They also considered a variation of an idea they had discussed before: setting up a new company to make a bid for all the shares in Celtic. The Celtic Investor Group would put in at least £2 million and offer either cash or shares in the new company in exchange for Celtic shares. They would wait for instructions from McCann and Dempsey before proceeding but the instruction was expected within ten days.

But before the instruction came, Low received a message on 14 February that was more welcome than any Valentine's card. Two Celtic directors wanted to talk. It was a dramatic turnaround. Not only were Chairman Kevin Kelly and stadium manager Tom Grant directors, they were members of a voting pact which legally bound five directors to act together. That pact of five had voted down the biggest ever offer of investment in a British football club. If that pact could be split, control of the club could be won.

It was the moment the rebels had been waiting for, only now there was a complication: the Haughey-Weisfeld bid. At least two of the five directors in the voting pact were ready to entertain offers, but Kelly and Grant were unwilling. In a mood approaching panic, they got a message through to the rebels they had scorned only weeks earlier.

Their approach came via a circuitous route. Kelly was an employee and director, though not a shareholder, of a small retail chain called The Trophy Centre. Its managing director and controlling shareholder was Jim Torbett, which effectively made him Kelly's boss. By the time the two directors asked for a meeting Dempsey was holidaying in Los Angeles, so Torbett contacted Brian's business partner, John Keane, in Edinburgh. The message was that the rebels had to put a deal together or Haughey and Weisfeld's offer would be accepted. The club was fast running out of money and time. It was on the brink of receivership.

A meeting was quickly arranged. In a once upper-class Glasgow Victorian townhouse in Royal Terrace, now converted to the offices of a firm called Standard Taverns, the two sides met. Torbett accompanied Kelly and Grant. Banker-turned-businessman Dominic Keane, and Low, were there for the rebels.

Kelly, balding and thin with the face of an ageing cherbub, and the stocky dark-haired Grant reported that they were coming under increasing pressure to accept the Haughey-Weisfeld bid. Kelly was upset because he was not convinced Weisfeld was 'a Celtic person'.

'That's an interesting point after all you've saide about us,' commented Low.

But Kelly, unfazed, said they were all good Celtic people there. The Celtic Chairman had meant Weisfeld was a relatively recent convery to Celtic fanaticism compared to everyone else there who had been almost born to it. One of the rebels' objections to Weisfeld was his intention to buy out the men they blamed for ruining the club. They would prefer the directors to get nothing, but Low and Keane did not put that suggestion to Kelly and Grant.

Haughey and Weisfeld's plan seemed to rest on trading out of the crisis. With the pact members gone, probably to be followed by the remaining two directors, Jim Farrell and Jack McGinn, they could bring in popular Celtic personalities such as Billy McNeill and Brian Dempsey. The financially damaging protests and drift away of supporters would be lifted, income would increase, prices might go up and they could renegotiate the club's borrowings with the bank.

Kelly and Grant were against the plan but given the club's financial problems they had no alternative of their own. Kelly asked if the rebels could put a deal together. Low said they could. Then he asked Kelly: 'Would you be prepared to support Fergus McCann and the proposals he put forward on 26 November if you could stay on the board?'

He would. The only other directors he would insist should stay on the board were Jack McGinn, who in two years was to become President of the Scottish Football Association – a useful appointment for Celtic – and Tom Grant. All the rest could go, including his cousin Michael.

Grant too would support the proposals but he wanted some job security. He would not insist on staying as a director, and he was prepared to sell 729 of his 1,729 shares, but he wanted a five-year contract as stadium manager.

With their agreement to McCann's proposals, Keane and Low began briefing the pair on how to defend themselves against the Weisfeld plan. Here was a member of the rebel investor group and one of its chief advisors now advising the club Chairman and a director on how to block a change of ownership . . . at least until the change they wanted could be brought about. And the weapon they were using against the other pact members was the very pact drawn up to foil the rebels.

The pact, officially called a shareholders' trust, took the form of a separate company called Celtic Nominees Ltd. It amounted to a detailed legal agreement binding together Kelly, Grant, Michael Kelly, club secretary Chris White, and deputy Chairman David Smith. It was dubbed by *The Herald*'s reporter Ian Paul 'the most infamous conspiracy since the Gunpowder Plot'. It had been designed to prevent any of its members selling out to the rebels. Any one of the five wanting to sell had first to offer his shares to the others in proportion to the number of shares they already held. It was soon to become a noose for them.

Smith, who had paid £250,000 for his shares, and White now wanted out. The others could not afford to buy their shares so the only was Smith and White could sell was to persuade the others to sell to Haughey and Weisfeld. Kevin

Kelly had the nerve to want the rebels to put up 3.6million in cash for him and Grant to pay Smith, White and cousin Michael £300 a share for their shares and their families' stakes. Low and Keane refrained from giving him their honest opinion of this suggestion but they did put up an alternative.

The rebels would finance Kelly and Grant to buy half the shares of any director who wanted to sell. This would effectively give the rebels control, it would block Haughey and Weisfeld and it would deny a fat profit to the directors they held responsible for the crisis. Low and Keane were turning the tables on the pact.

Grant was asked to get a copy from David Smith of the offer, and a copy of the voting pact Smith had signed, just in case any changes had crept in since the one Grant had signed. Any discrepancy might be exploited. The first test of Kelly and Grant's courage came sooner than expected. On the afternoon of Friday, 18 February, an agitated Tom Grant rang Low. He had just been telephoned by Smith.

All the pact members were being asked to go to the offices of Dickson Minto in Edingburgh at 6.30 p.m. Dickson Minto are a firm of high-powered lawyers, with a formidable reputation in business takeovers and buy-outs. The pact directors were supposed to go there to discuss the offer from Weisfeld. What should Grant do?

Five members of a Glasgow-based company – Celtic – were supposed to go to the Edinburgh offices of a firm of corporate lawyers to 'discuss' an offer. And at short notice. It didn't add up. The Haughey-Weisfeld offer amounted to £300 a share. For White, that meant £887,100. For Smith, £285,000. That added up.

'I don't think you're being summoned to this meeting to discuss the Weisfeld offer,' Low told Grant, 'especially not at Dickson Minto's offices, especially not at short notice. I think you're going to be stramrollered into accepting the offer. Use the short notice as an excuse not to go.'

Grant told Smith he couldn't make it. So did Kelly. Smith called Grant back to say it was extremely important they go to Edinburgh because the club's bank, the Bank of Scotland, were saying they couldn't guarantee cheques or cover the wages. But Grant and Kelly held out. Eventually Michael Kelly decided not to go either. The meeting did not take place.

Low's suspicions were confirmed when he later learned Haughey was waiting in an adjoining room at Dickson Minto, with champagne ready to be opened in celebration. Weisfeld had not gone only because he had accepted a personal invitation to meet Prime Minister John Major, at an exclusive reception and gala dinner in Glasgow.

The rebels had now won a little time to muster their forces, which were spread between Scotland, Arizona where McCann was staying at his summer home, and California where Dempsey was staying with friends. But they would not have long. Kelly and Grant were openly anxious, with good reason. After all, they were directors of a company facing receivership yet they had just turned their backs on more than £500,000 each. They had to be reassured they would be taken care of, that the rebels would fund they buying of shares from the other directors.

The rebels' immediate problem, though, was to fend off Haughey and Weisfeld. Since the earlier meeting there had been continuing telephone calls between Scotland, Arizona and California. With the time differences involved there was little chance of sleep. Calls and faxes would go out from Glasgow until around 2 a.m. only for incoming calls and faxes to begin around 6 a.m. Underlying all this telecommunications traffic was the message that Weisfeld's bid to buy out the failed directors had to be blocked. Weisfeld had been stopped once, but he was not a man to give up easily.

Low and Keane had to fend him off and preserve the status quo until McCann and Dempsey could put their own plan into effect. Both were making arrangements to return. Given Celtic's financial situation, given that Kevin Kelly and Tom Grant would at last now support them, along with Farrell and possibly McGinn, given the supporters' attitude, they could win total victory . . . if they could fend off Haughey and Weisfeld.

At 7 p.m. on Sunday, 20 February, another meeting was helf at Royal Terrace. Low and Keane warned Kelly and Grant that they were going to come under enormous pressure. They would be asked for personal guarantees. As shareholders in a limited company, they were liable only for the value of their shares, although if Celtic went under,

Grant stood to lose his job. Their personal finances, their homes and cars were safe. A personal gurantee would change that. They would be asked to guarantee Celtic's debt to the bank, and if the club couldn't pay it their homes and savings would be at risk.

Grant brought a copy of the pact Smith had signed, but it was exactly the same as earlier versions, which Keane and Low had already seen. However, they were amazed when they saw the document containing the offer to buy the shares of all the directors in the pact. It did not name any of the individuals making the offer. According to this document, the offer came from two companies, called Jean Armour plc and Newbyquest, and an unnamed customer of the Bank of Scotland. Jean Armour plc was believed to be an owner and operator of public houses and Newbyquest was a company bought 'off-the-shelf'. If you want to set up a company quickly you can buy one ready-made from a specialist agent, often with the meaningless name he has already given it, like Newbyquest.

With this offer was a letter from the Bank of Scotland at 110 St Vincent Street, Glasgow, to say that their unnamed customer had deposited £1.8 million with them in support of the offer which was worth £3.6 million. It said also that another of their customers had been given a facility of £900,000 and that an unnamed customer of the Royal Bank of Scotland who was known to be of good standing had a facility of £900,000. In short, half of the offer was being made with borrowed funds.

Here were the Chairman and directors of a limited company being asked to accept an offer fron unnamed individuals with borrowed money, without seeing a business plan and without meeting the would-be buyers. At its very best, it was a long way from normal business practice and was unexpected from Smith, a man who must have been familiar with financial practice. Low and Keane were not inclined to view it as its very best. In fact, Low laughed out loud at it.

Smith had said that the Bank of Scotland were going to bounce Celtic's cheques. Kelly was told to ring the Bank next morning and find out if it was true. If it was, they would know the problem they had to deal with and could put together a defence strategy. If it were not true, Kelly would ask for Smith's resignation.

Kelly was told by the Bank that Smith had been telling the truth. The club had run out of money. The directors had broken the terms of the overdraft facility. The next day the Bank sent a letter requesting personal guarantees to cover the overdraft.

The day that letter was sent Smith set up another meeting of the pact to discuss the offer. He, White and Michael Kelly were prepared to sell, but Kevin Kelly and Grant were not. Smith could not deliver a deal to Weisfeld. Then Kevin and Tom sprang the surprise prepared by Low and Keane. Not only would they not sell their shares, they were prepared to buy shared from those who were. They could not afford the shares themselves so Smith must have known they were in league with the rebels and wer now being financed by them. He would know, too, it was the other David, Low, giving them the instructions. They were like two corporate gunfighters, quick on the deal, trying to out-draw each other.

Willie Haughey, however, was not one of them. Successful and affable, he was still no match for the corporate specialists. He was allowed to believe his deal with the pact was still on and he reported this faithfully to Weisfeld. He also reported it to the Press.

Weisfeld, having been told he could get the pact's 42 per cent to add to his own ten per cent in the club, at one point even discussed inviting Dempsey to become its Chairman, though he was honest enough to admit he would like the post himself. All along Dempsey had been the people's champion. His pronouncements had been calm and considered, delivered in the statesman-like tone Members of Parliament aspire to, unconsciously learned from his own politician father. Throughout he had kept faith with the supporters and they put their trust in him. Dempsey remained non-committal.

Believing he had a deal to take over Celtic, Weisfeld left for a holiday in Australia. A few days later he telephoned his grandson, Michael McDonald Jr, at his home in Bothwell, just south of Glasgow, to say he was the new boss of Celtic. The young boy took up the refrain, repeatedly chanting:

'Papa's the boss.' Had Weisfeld stayed, the result just might have been different. The deal did not happen because his allies misread the situation. For the second time he had been blocked. When he learned this, his anger was outdone only by his wife Vera's and it was aimed at Smith while his frustration was aimed at Haughey. He complained to Dempsey that someone was feeding him wrong information. He asked Kevin Kelly to name his price but Kelly said his shares were not for sale for any sum.

The directors who wanted to sell were no happier. Smith had paid most for his shares, around £250,000. He knew now he was dealing with the McCann-Dempsey camp and Kevin Kelly and Tom Grant were now taking advice from the very people the pact had been doggedly fighting off for two years. His main potential buyer, Weisfeld, was furious, the Bank wanted personal guarantees from the directors and the media wanted to know what was going on. Something had to be done.

Dempsey arrived back on Glasgow on Thursday, 24 February. He said truthfully that neither he nor McCann would make a move unless invited to by two or more directors, but they already had the invitation. 'Celtic cannot go on hurting themselves,' he said. 'We cannot put everybody through an EGM again without some assurances that the board want it.'

Nobody wanted another bruising extraordinary general meeting. One witness to the November meeting said it had been so stressful that Michael Kelly and Chris White had looked drained afterwards. Yet the rebels were in no mood to buy out them or any other directors. They wanted to invest in the club, not in the people who had run the club into its current position. Dempsey refused to criticise Haughey and Weisfeld for putting up millions 'to do what they think is best for Celtic' but he lambasted Smith, White and especially Michael Kelly.

On the evening he returned, even before going home to his family, Dempsey went to the City Halls in Glasgow to address a meeting of 1,000 supporters of Celts For Change. This pressure group had been formed only four months before by a handful of supporters, including Matt McGlone, editor of the fanzine *Once A Tim*. In little more than eight weeks they had attracted a support of 8,000, but they had been holding their ultimate weapon, a match boycott, in reserve as a last resort. Now they were calling for a boycott of Saturday's game against Kilmarnock.

Dempsey was given a standing ovation. He had been fighting for three years to effect change, to save Celtic from the looming catastrophe which had been visible all that time to those who would see it. The son of a politician, he had contributed political as well as business skills to the rebels' campaign. At times the restraint of his public utterances had frustrated some journalists impatient to turn the Celtic saga into a simple revenge story. One exasperated wag dubbed him 'Saint Brian'. He insisted he had come reluctantly into the limelight. Like Julius Ceasar, he kept declining the crown the crowd wanted to put on his head. Now he stood before the crowd to take the well-earned applause. He described the behaviour of the directors as 'grotesque', and 'a tragedy, a deceit, and a betrayal'.

He now backed a boycott. The Affiliation of Registered Supporters Clubs, which had 12,000 members, had decided they would either stay away from the Kilmarnock game or leave after 60 minutes. Celts For Change had been arguing against that tactic on financial and safety grounds: it would not deprive the board of income, and it might lead to scuffles with supporters who disagreed with it. The Association of Celtic Supporters Clubs, the official body, could not urge a boycott because of their constitution, but many of its members also belonged to Celts For Change. The boycott was intended to hit the board hard after months of protests and demonstrations had failed to bring change at the top.

Celtic needed an average attendance of 20,000 per game just to stop sinking further into debt. Because of cancellations due to increasingly unpredicatable winter weather, they had not had a home match form more than a month, and they were not due another one until they met Motherwell in late March. Gates had been hovering just below that figure, sinking to 16,654 when they last met Motherwell in November. The big matches, of course, brought in more but no more were due that season.

McCann might have been out of the country but he was not out of reach. He faxed the Bank of Scotland to accuse them of pressuring Kevin Kelly to sell his shares to unnamed customers of the Bank. He warned of the poor view Celtic supporters would take of the Bank, and of legal action against directors who did sell by shareholders who might feel excluded from the chance to sell their shares.

He then offered to buy Celtic's debt to the bank of £5 million, less the equivalent of 18 months interest, to guarantee another £1 million overdraft, and to raise £17.8 million in cash to invest in the club. This would, he said, bring 'a prompt and beneficial end to the uncertainty in the community surrounding the fate of Celtic'.

As an additional incentive, he added: 'This offer may be withdrawn at any time'. The Bank denied his accusation and said they could not transfer the club's debt to anyone without the approval of the board.

Smith, though, had one last surprise to spring. On the morning of Friday, 25 February, Mike Stanger, a director of Michael Kelly's public relations firm, rounded up journalists for a Press conference at Parkhead. Not only sports reporters but business journalists were summoned too. It was a hurriedly convened affair. Francis Shennan, a freelance business writer who, with *Scotland on Sunday*'s football correspondent Kevin McCarra, had broken the story of the Celtic takeover plan two years earlier, was given 90 minutes notice. Alf Young, Economics Editor of *The Herald*, received the phone call while in the shower.

The entrance to the Jock Stein Lounge at Parkhead is dominated by a portrait of Celtic's most successful manager, spotlit and flanked by green drapes. In the lounge the journalists speculated about the announcement to come during the short wait for the news conference to start. If the board were selling out, the Press would not have been summouned. They could possibly be announcing the arrival of a new investor but it was doubtful.

Kevin Kelly and Smith walked briskly through the lounge to take their seats in front of their audience. Apart from the briefest of introductions, Kelly said nothing. This was Smith's show. His body language was defensive, with his arms frequently folded across his chest, but he also leaned forward in an assertive mood.

What he had to announce was that 'cornerstone' funding

of £20 million had been committed for a 'state-of-the-art' stadium complex at Cambuslang, that notice would be given the following week of an EGM to authorise the issue of 25,000 shares raising up to £6 million, that the club would go public with a Stock Exchange listing by the end of the year, and that a new board would be appointed for Celtic plc, although the existing directors might continue to serve on a separate club board.

At this point Patrick Nally, who ran an Oxford-based consultancy with the overly clever name of StadiVarius, was wheeled on to give more details of the funding. It was, he said, part of a £65 million package for a string of stadia to be built around Britain, which could include deals with Derby County and Sunderland football clubs. The backers were to recoup their investment by selling to drinks and food companies like Coca-Cola or Pepsi the exclusive right to have their products sold within the complexes.

'Glasgow will be the *blue riband* of six stadia to be built throughout the UK,' he said. 'The funding is for a network of stadia: Glasgow, Sunderland, Derby, the south coast, the west of England and one close to London. The group working with us is committed to the whole network.'

Here was news of what, if it materialised, would be a mammoth British construction project being announced, not in the City of London, but at Parkhead. Nally did not immediately volunteer the name of the backers but in response to a question said it was Gefinor. The journalists' response was: 'Who?' and 'Could you spell that?'

The tone of the Michael Kelly Press release which accompanied the announcement was little short of euphoric. 'Celtic confirms 21st century vision,' it read. 'Far-reaching proposals to transcend factions.' The plan was 'a comprehensive and visionary package of radical measures designed to take the club into a glittering new future in the 21st century'. In case the journalists were still not sure it was good news, the four main points of the announcement had a smiling cartoon face printed beside them.

It described Gefinor as an international merchant bank. Even the business journalists had not heard of them. Questions to Nally elicited the fact that this was not 'cornerstone' funding, after all, more like 'rooftop' funding at

26

best. It was at most a commitment to underwrite any shortfall in the cost of a new stadium. If Celtic did not raise £30 million, Gefinor's supposed funding would not be there.

Cambuslang, originally designed as a 'doughnut-shaped' stadium, was now a rectangular 40,000-seat stadium alongside a 10,000-seat indoor areana. 'The building will be speeded up,' said Michael Kelly afterwards. 'It is a simpler construction.'

The news conference split up into individual interviews for television and radio. While David Smith was giving an interview to Chick Young of BBC Scotland, Chick's mobile phone rang. It was Willie Haughey asking Young if he knew anything about a rumoured announcement. Chick said he could ask Smith himself and passed the phone over. On camera, Smith had to try to calm an irate Haughey. 'I'm sorry you feel that way,' said Smith languidly as he leaned his chair back on two legs.

Haughey was not the only one taken by surprise – the Press conference *preceded* a board meeting to inform the directors. Celtic director Jimmy Farrell rang Low that morning, about an hour after the Press conference began. Low had to tell him about the announcement. He also had to tell Farrell about the Bank's letter to Chris White as company secretary a week earlier and what it said. Weisfeld was a little better informed. Smith had faxed him a copy of the Press release 12 hours before it was issued in Glasgow.

A second briefing for the three business journalists there revealed that any commitment was not directly to Celtic but to StadiVarius. Gefinor, it seems, had been established 30 years ago with Middle Eastern money. They had invested heavily in New York property. They were, said Smith, a 'substantial organisation' with $300 million of shareholders' funds. Only after the media briefing did he go along to the Bank of Scotland with details of the plan, though they were, he said 'aware of it'.

The announcement inspired little confidence among either the business or the sports journalists, and it did even less for the long-suffering players. 'What we have heard is business jargon that means nothing to the ordinary man in the street,' Charlie Nicholas told Hugh Keevins of *The Scotsman*. 'The fans are confused and so are the players.'

Celtic players too had been hoping for changes on the board. They had returned from training to see disappointed fans outside the club and had to send captain Paul McStay to ask for a meeting with the directors. 'Whether it is football or finance, it is easy to talk a good game,' said Nicholas.

The fans were distinctly unimpressed. Celts for Change declared they boycott was still on. Peter Rafferty, leader of the Affiliation of Registered Celtic Supporters' Clubs, who had not missed a game by choice for more than 30 years, said nothing had changed. He was 'more unconvinced' than before. Only the President of the Celtic Supporters' Association, Jim Brodie, hoped fans would now change their minds.

Next day's newspapers greeted the announcement with a mixture of surprise, confusion and disbelief. Colin McSeveney of *The Herald* had telephoned Gefinor's London office only to speak to an answering machine that did not work properly. Edinburgh money managers who ran a unit trust for Gefinor knew nothing about such plans and said the deal was 'not their scene at all'. *The Sun* splashed its own view of Smith and his accomplices: Park-heid Cases! Hours later Allan Caldwell reported in Glasgow's *Evening Times* that Gefinor was not registered with the Bank of England as allowed to practise in the UK and it had resigned from the Investment Management Regulatory Organisation (IMRO), the main investment watchdog body in Britain.

Only the snow came to the board's aid to spare them the embarrassment of the boycott by forcing the game against Kilmarnock to be called off. Instead of a demonstration, a hearse arrived at Parkhead. The *Sunday Mail* were setting up a picture for next day's paper under a green headline: 'Celtic RIP'.

Smith might have thought his hastily arranged stalling tactic would throw the rebels into confusion and weaken their position, at least temporarily. After all, how could they vote against the issue of 25,000 new shares when they had been consistently calling for a share issue themselves? He claimed he had buyers already lined up for most of the new shares. But he was really weakening the fragile branch on which he had already crawled too far out. McCann and Dempsey, joined by the furious Weisfeld, were ready to demand that the new shares should be issued to the fans rather than the anonymous financial institutions Smith might invite in.

The rebels were prepared to underwrite the share issue. This meant they would guarantee all the new shares would be sold, because they would buy any shares the fans did not want or could not afford. It was a no-lose strategy. The fans who bought the shares were likely to be rebel supporters, and the rebel leaders would increase their stakes by buying what was left. If Smith refused this offer, the rebels had a justification for voting against his share issue. A new issue of shares needed a two-thirds majority – or 66.7 per cent – and Smith could count on no more than 60 per cent from the voting pact and their relations. The rebels would therefore need only 33.4 per cent to stop it, and his fragile plan would collapse like a house of cards. It had no chance of passing its second hurdle, a flotation on the Stock Exchange. Celtic's financial position was so poor the club would not win a Stock Market listing. Manchester United had, it is true, gone to market but they already had a modern stadium and a sound financial base.

Smith's supposed package did not even last a week. Within days the *Evening Times* splashed another Caldwell story under the headline 'What £20m?'. Gefinor now denied committing any money to Cambuslang. Michael Kelly embarked on a damage-limitation exercise, insisting the facts supported the announcement of the previous Friday. But by then events had moved on.

On the Monday Smith told all the directors the club was nearly finished and he would visit the Bank. General manager Roland Mitchell did not want to put Celtic into receivership but he did want the Bank's problem solved. The Bank wanted personal guarantees and the directors' shares as collateral for the debt. Putting up the shares as collateral or pledging them in any way would have broken the terms of the voting pact. This would have allowed those who wanted to sell a way out. Two days later the six other directors went to the Bank. Mitchell told the directors the club was going into receivership unless they gave personal guarantees and pledged their shares. He set a deadline of 3.30 p.m. the next day.

The team were also leaving things to the last minute. That night John Collins scored the only goal of the match against Kilmarnock from a free kick in the 89th minute. The game marked the beginning – and as it turned out – the end of the boycott. Celts For Change had even paid for an independent research company to monitor the attendance. The official attendance was 10,822, the wortst attended game at Parkhead for six years. Celts For Change, knowing that many season ticket holders had stayed away and estimating the Kilmarnock support at 2,000, put the Celtic attendance at only 8,225. Paul McStay stayed away – but he had been sent home with 'flu symptoms threequarters of an hour before the match.

After 60 minutes another 300 fans walked out, jeered at by the supporters who stayed. Before they left the only light-hearted moment of the match came when a fox ran out of the east terracing, across the pitch and into the west terracing. The fans started chanting derisively: 'One Michael Kelly, there's only one Michael Kelly!' *Herald* football writer Jim Traynor reported one fan shouting: 'That's all we need. We've got a board full of Basil Fawltys and now we've got a Basil Brush on the pitch.'

Added to their running boycott of the club newspaper, *Celtic View*, Celts for Change estimated the cost to the club at £300,000.

Andrew Smith, editor of *Celtic View*, had planned that week's front page on the Gefinor story with the headline 'We Will Deliver.' Smith ordered him to change it to 'Help Us Deliver' – not the most confident of messages. The deputy Chairman had also asked Andrew to send him questions on the announcement so he could answer them in the paper. 'Make them difficult ones,' he said confidently.

One of the questions faxed to him asked why directors Jimmy Farrell and Jack McGinn had not been informed of the announcement before the media. The question was never answered and did not appear in the paper. After he had put the *View* to bed that week, Smith was speaking to a reporter from *The Sun*. 'You can have this on the record,' he said 'but I feel like Goebbels tonight.' *The Sun* ran the story and Smith honestly believed he had thrown away his job – but the tide happened to be turning in his favour.

Weisfeld flew back to Scotland in the morning of the day that threatened to be Celtic's last before the receivers were called in. He had been authorised by Smith to speak to the Bank about Celtic and the suntanned but jet-lagged businessman went straight there. Mitchell and Weisfeld believed he was there with the full knowledge and authority of the board. Weisfeld agreed to put up a personal guarantee for £3 million of the £5.2 million overdraft. He left the Bank believing, for the third time, that he owned Celtic. He had flown into the country and in little more than minutes, he believed, he had pulled off the deal.

What he did not know was that just then eight men were meeting a short distance away in the offices of Pannell Kerr Forster. Brian Dempsey, Dominic Keane, Low and accountant Charles Barnett were sitting down with Kevin Kelly, Tom Grant, Jimmy Farrell and Jack McGinn – in short, a majority of the board of Celtic Football Club.

They knew they had to act. Unaware of Weisfeld's visit to the Bank, they believed they had less than six hours to save the club. Keane, an experienced banker himself, accompanied the four directors to the Bank while Low and Barnett spent the rest of the day putting an action plan together.

Keane and the directors reached the Bank at noon. Mitchell was stunned. The directors told him they had been kept in the dark. Because they were a majority of the board, they could overrule the arrangement reached only an hour earlier with Weisfeld. But Mitchell told them they would have to come up with an alternative or the club was going into receivership. He gave them until 4.30 p.m. to give him their plans and until noon the next day to find £1 million or an equivalent guarantee, with further guarantees to be found the next week.

Around 2.30 p.m. the directors and Keane returned to Pannell Kerr Forster where they put a Fergus McCann plan into action. The four directors called a board meeting for 3.30 p.m., only an hour before the Bank's first deadline expired. With the club's fate hanging in the balance, McGinn said he could stay for only an hour because he was to go to Zurich on SFA business. Faxes were sent to Michael Kelly Associates, Cannon Street Investments in London where Smith was based, and to Chris White at Parkhead. Michael

Kelly said he could not be there before 5 p.m. Smith and White did not respond.

At the board meeting the four directors voted to strip White and Smith of all executive responsibilities with immediate effect. White was suspended on full pay. The directors also demanded their immediate resignations. Then the board agreed to accept £1 million from the McCann team. The board meeting was adjourned: Mitchell had to be faxed by 4.30 p.m. The fax was sent with minutes to spare.

Letters were sent by courier to Smith's home in Putney and White's home in Whitecraigs, Glasgow, telling them they had been stripped of executive responsibility and demanding their immediate resignations. It was all done by five pm. Celtic had been reprieved from receivership – for 19 hours at least. But delivering £1 million by the high noon deadline of next day would not be so easy.

The Press had heard something was going on. Calls were coming in. In the first public sign that a change of régime was imminent a Celtic Press release was put out, not by Michael Kelly Associates, but by the rebels' PR firm, Charles Barker Scotland Ltd. Michael Kelly telephoned about an hour later to be told what was happening. He was furious. Smith telephoned Weisfeld that night. A stunned Weisfeld realised the prize had been snatched from him for a third time.

At 8 a.m next day Low was in Dempsey's office to plan their strategy. It was agreed John Keane in Edinburgh would provide the £1 million guarantee. Celtic's stay of execution had less than four hours to run.

Keane phoned the Bank of Ireland in Glasgow but the paperwork involved in a guarantee is more difficult than for a cash deposit. It would not go through in the three hours remaining.

Dominic Keane was at Parkhead. A board meeting had been called for 10 a.m. Reporters had assembled in a room set aside on the first floor where the tea and coffee provided soon ran out as their wait went on. Outside the photographers and cameramen had to brave a cold west wind.

The first fans, drawn by the morning's Press reports and the desire to catch even a fleeting glimpse of football history, started to assemble. Their number grew gradually but steadily all day. It was like a scene from a science fiction film where people are drawn to a place by a power they cannot explain. They waited with the patience, if not quite the reverence, of a crowd keeping vigil during the election of a new Pope.

McCann had arranged for £1 million in dollars to be wired from New York to London but it had still to be converted into pounds and transmitted on to the Clydesdale Bank in St Vincent Street. Low met him off the plane from the States and rushed him to Dempsey's office for 9.30 a.m. The million had still not reached Glasgow. Two and a half hours to go.

At 10 a.m. they rang the Clydesdale. The money had just arrived. McCann, Low and Barnett raced to the Bank. From there they phoned the Bank of Scotland just along the road. How did they want the money? Cheque or banker's draft? Payable to whom? At last they walked briskly to the Bank of Scotland to meet Mitchell and Douglas Henderson, Divisional General Manager of UK Banking. They started to fill in the paperwork that goes with a cheque for £1 million.

Low lifted his head after adding his signature as a witness to the transaction. It was 11.52 a.m. on Friday, 4 March 1994. The nightmare was over. A disastrous dynasty had been ended. A new, more professional generation had taken over. Celtic Football Club had been saved . . . at exactly eight minutes to noon.

But the takeover was far from over . . .

Chapter Two

THE ORIGINAL SIN

They end up paying £2 million for a waste site at Cambuslang
when they could have had 14 acres at Robroyston for £1.25
million and they would have had a tax gain.

— Brian Dempsey about Celtic's board

I

THE journey that McCann and Low had to make from the
Bank of Scotland to Parkhead was only a few miles, but in
spirit it was a world and a century away. St Vincent Street is
in the heart of Glasgow's commercial centre where opulent
banking halls are testament to the city's former role as the
Second City of the Empire. Today the banking halls are still
busy but behind those fine cornices now run the computer
cables that modern money management demands. Financial
services had provided increased employment during
Glasgow's revival after the collapse of traditional heavy
industry.

Parkhead had never been an opulent part of the city. It had
been a village of weavers' cottages but in the mid-19th
century mechanical mills had impoverished the weavers and
swollen the city so that it absorbed the little village. By the
end of the 19th century the city had been swollen still further
by waves of Irish imigrants. Poor, hungry and hated because

in desperation they would take jobs at lower wages than the native Scots, they huddled into ghettos, falling back on the only consolations they had: family, religion and often drink.

But by that time, too, some of the immigrants had risen beyond labouring jobs, into shop-keeping, tailoring and other trades. These men frequently became stalwarts of parish committees and the parish of St Mary's had a group of particularly resourceful men. In February 1887 they saw the Irish Catholic football club Hibernian, from Edinburgh, defeat Dumbarton in the Scottish Cup final. At a reception afterwards Hibs' secretary John McFadden had urged Glasgow Catholics to follow his club's example.

In the audience was the headmaster of Sacred Heart School, Brother Walfrid, a member of the Marist religious order. He had organised a Poor Children's Dinner Table to make sure children had one hot meal a day. Far from St Vincent Street, the children relied on the hard-pressed Catholic charity, the St Vincent de Paul Society. Brother Walfrid saw a Catholic football team in Glasgow as a source of raising both funds and morale. A successful team could encourage the immigrants to aspire to success for themselves.

Eight months after Hibs had stirred up this ambition, Celtic Football and Athletic Club was founded. Within a week it had leased six acres of ground. Within two months 45 people had pledged financial support, including 20 shillings from the Archbishop. And only four months after that the club had a ground with an open-air stand – beneath which were two dressing-rooms with showers, and rooms for trainer and referee – and a mound for terracing. The spirit of 1888 contrasted sharply with the failure of spirit and enterprise in the 1990s.

True, the costs of re-building Parkhead today, or building anew at Robroyston or Cambuslang, would stun the club's founders. But considering the poor resources they had, and the number of wealthy supporters who offered investment in the 1990s, it is clear something had been lost from the club by the time the takeover plan had been launched.

On 28 May 1888 the Celtic team took the field against their first ever opponents, Rangers. The Old Firm was born. The joining of these two teams in rivalry has had a profound effect on players and fans. But it had a more unpredicatble effect. The rivalry reached right to the top. The boards of both clubs would forever watch what the other was doing. A hundred years later it would tempt a Celtic board of directors into trying to emulate their Rangers rivals. As on the field, however, you need players suited to the tactics you adopt. The unsuitability of the board for those tactics cost them the club.

From the first 5-2 win over Rangers, Celtic established themselves almost at once as a force in Scottish football, reaching the Scottish Cup final in only their first season. In the club's first eight years it won the Charity Cup for five years running, the Glasgow Cup three times and the Scottish Cup once, as well as three League championships. In fact, in one season – only the club's third – it won the Scottish, Charity and Glasgow Cup, prompting Celtic committee member Ned McGinn to telegraph the Pope with the news. The Pontiff failed to reply.

Just as important in explaining the history that followed is the kind of support Celtic excited. The team reached three of the five Scottish Cup finals between 1889 and 1893. When Celtic played in the final the average attendance was 24,000. In the finals without Celtic, the average gate was only 11,600. More than a footballing force had been born: a fanatical following had appeared almost from nowhere and, even in the leanest years, would never fully desert the team.

The emotions the club could evoke, at all levels of society, would result in 1994 with three millionaires wanting to put money into what was – in strictly business terms – a little near-bankrupt company in the east end of Glasgow.

Sporting success and the support were there from the beginning, but the tight control of three families was not. Dr Hugh Drake, a descendant of one of the first committee men, pointed out: 'You will find something like 15 men holding the destiny of Celtic in their hands. It was only in the years that followed that we tend to get this power shift of gravity away from the many.'

II

WHEN Celtic met Aberdeen on 2 May 1990 for their last league game, it marked the end of a less than memorable season. But they still had the chance of a place in the UEFA Cup the following season and when Andy Walker put them 1-0 up in the first half most of the 20,154 spectators were delighted.

But during the second 45 minutes the crowd had to watch a team unravelling before their eyes as the let Aberdeen first equalise and then humiliate them with two additional goals. It left Celtic with 34 points, 16 behind leage leaders Rangers who still had a game in hand. Asssistant manager Tommy Craig was so distracted when he left the ground, he walked five yards ahead of his wife without noticing. 'I'm just glad to see the league season over,' said manager Billy McNeill.

Unfortunately ten days later they lost to Aberdeen in the Tennent's Scottish Cup, ending the season without any trophies.

Off the field the club had problems too. Financially successful clubs have the resources to build repeatedly successful teams and Celtic were slipping down the commercial league as well as the Football League. The Government's adoption of *The Taylor Report* which followed the Hillsborough disaster in England when Liverpool fans were crushed to death, would make all-seater stadia compulsory for Scottish Premier League clubs by 1 August 1994. Arch-rivals Rangers already had a superb stadium and were threatening to leave Celtic behind financially. The foundations had been laid by Lawrence Marlborough who had brought in Graeme Souness to lay the team foundations. Reaching too far a little too fast for his finances, Marlborough had been forced to sell and it was Souness who interested David Murray in buying. Souness in turn had handed over to Walter Smith. Now they were leading the league by a comfortable six points from their nearest challengers, Aberdeen, and they still had money to spend.

The day after the league game against Aberdeen, Celtic brought an entrepreneur of their own on to the board. It was a break with tradition, at least with the tradition since the Kelly and White families seized control for themselves. Celtic directors were usually either related to one of these families or worked their way through the ranks at the club. Suddenly, an outsider was being invited in.

Brian Dempsey was a property developer and house-builder who had built up his business from nothing. He had already been advising the directors in a private capacity and had first been approached to join the board in February that year. He was a Lanarkshire man and was the son of Jimmy Dempsey, the Labour MP for Coatbridge and Airdrie. As a boy he had accompanied his father on his campaigns, often asking afterwards why he had used a particular phrase. He had absorbed a great deal from his father, consciously and unconsciously. When he stood to address public meetings later in the Celtic campaign, he would often stand with his left hand holding the fingers of his right. His mother told him the stance was exactly the same as his father's, but he had no conscious memory of it.

The young Dempsey loved music, played several instruments and once thought of teaching music. There may still be a part of his personality that will only be satisfied by teaching or campaigning for a political cause, but the poverty of the family's circumstances drove him into business. Many millionaires, whether they realise it or not, go into business for more than profit. Money becomes a symbol for what they lacked in early life. Ask Dempsey why he went into business and he will say: 'Because we had nothing.'

He had been with Salvesen Homes when he decided to go out on his own. By his mid-forties he was a millionaire. Given his wealth, he drove a modest car and lived in a modest home, or rather a series of them, in Scotland, Ireland and latterly one in Florida. By any material standards he was a success. But if you were the type who believed Man cannot avoid his fate, you might see what followed as Dempsey having a cause thrust upon him. At the time, though, he was seen simply as a man with the kind of skills needed to oversee the redevelopment of a stadium or the building of a new one.

Co-opted on to the board with him was Michael Kelly. He was the better known of the pair. He had been Lord Provost (or mayor) at the time of the *Glasgow's Miles Better* campaign. The campaign, put together by the city's leading advertising man at that time, John Struthers of Struthers Advertising, changed the city's image forever. Its logo, the Mr Happy cartoon character created by Roger Hargreaves, smiled from stone-cleaned buildings, posters and books, effectively laughing away the old *No Mean City* image. The deliberately ambiguous logo declared that Glasgow was better than it was and better than many other places once considered superior.

The thin, bearded face of the city's first citizen, Dr Michael Kelly, became as familiar as Mr Happy. A Labour councillor and later a CBE, a PhD and a lecturer in economics, trim and articulate, he was as much a symbol of the changing city. The list of letters after his name stretched halfway across the foot of his company notepaper. This was no traditional Labour politician from the once Red Clydeside. He could be safely allowed to speak from any national or international platform, and he did, advising other cities such as Cardiff which were anxious to undergo a similar metamorphosis. When he left office, after a brief flirtation with Scottish Television, he set up Michael Kelly Associates, which quickly became the largest independent public relations company in Scotland with offices in Glasgow and Edinburgh.

Kelly was therefore seen as the man with the public relations skills to market the club. And, unlike Dempsey, he fitted the Celtic tradition: his grandfather was James Kelly, captain of the first Celtic team and later Chairman of the club. Where football helped James Kelly to rise from apprentice joiner to Justice of the Peace and social status, Michael Kelly had acquired the social status and position as JP on his way to the board of a football club. But his arrival on the board had a use beyond his PR role. Company secretary Chris White did not want Dempsey but he was outnumbered by the rest of the board. He agreed to Dempsey if he could bring in an ally at the same time. Kelly could support White and the family shareholders.

Dempsey did not know it but his tenure as a director was doomed to be only five months. In that time White and Kelly mustered shareholder support and marshalled proxy votes, while fellow directors remained unaware of what was to happen.

The two men joined a board which was ageing and ill-equipped to operate successfully in the modern commercial world that top-flight football was now part of. Chairman Jack McGinn had been the first editor of the *Celtic View* when the club decided to launch their own paper in 1965. Jimmy Farrell, a lawyer in his late sixties, had been on the board for a quarter of a century and before that had founded the Celtic Development Fund. Kevin Kelly was a director of the small but successful Trophy Centre group of shops. Only the club secretary, Christopher White, son of the late Chairman Desmond White, and Tom Grant were a similar age to Michael Kelly and Dempsey.

At the time Michael Kelly joined the Celtic board one of his clients was a company called Bremner, whose chairman was David Low. The Bremner experience had a direct effect on what was to happen at Parkhead. The unfolding of the Celtic story, with the diversions, distractions and deceptions subtracted, followed the pattern set by Bremner. The recruiting of shareholder support, obtaining irrevocable commitments or proxy votes, building up your backing before showing your hand, requistioning an EGM, using clauses of the Companies Acts and the company's consti-tution like artillery shells . . . all these were used to win Celtic.

Bremner had once owned a major Glasgow department store but it had been closed leaving the company little more than a shell which owned a firm of stockbrokers and, more importantly, a lot of cash. For years two groups had waged a bitter battle, sometimes using the courts, for control of the firm. Finally in 1989 the group led by a previous Chairman, Bournemouth-based businessman Jim Rowland-Jones, unseated the then Chairman, Dennis McGuinness.

It was the final straw for some of the Scottish financial community. There was now a threat that the Stock Exchange would strip Bremner of its stock market listing. Stock market listings were expensive and difficult to come by. Four firms of stockbrokers started recruiting Bremner shareholders who were tired of the apparently endless in-fighting. One of those behind the move was Low, then head of investment at the stockbrokers Torrie & Co in Edingburgh.

The stockbrokers 'four just men', as they liked to think of themselves, gathered irrevocable commitments from the shareholders to support the group's plans. When they had the support of more than 40 per cent of the shareholding, they requisitioned an extraordinary general meeting. Both sides relied heavily on the law, using clauses of the

Companies Acts. When it arrived, the EGM was one of the longest shareholders' meetings in Scottish business history. All the directors were voted out and a new board of professional advisors were voted in, with Low as Chairman.

In the meantime the shares had been suspended from the Stock Exchange because the company was no more han a shell. Low's job was to get a good deal for the shareholders. Over the next few months he turned the company into an investment trust, renamed it the Scottish Value Trust and had it re-listed on the Exchange. He and all but one of the professional advisors then resigned, having found independent directors to take over. One, Colin McLean, with shareholders' approval, remained to manage the investment of the company's funds. In its first six months of trading the new Trust outperformed the *FT* All-Share Index and the average of all investment trusts.

Low was a lifelong Celtic supporter but had never felt the need to be one of the 'in-crowd'. He did not hang out with the businessmen who frequented Parkhead or know any of the corporate heavyweights. Going to the game with pals he had known for years was a break from business. The pals might now mean with lawyers and accountants but they were there only for the football. Until he read of Dempsey and Kelly's co-option he had paid no attention to the business side.

The next time Low saw Kelly he wished him good luck and said Celtic would need his and Dempsey's skills. In the meantime he had another two months of battling to bring Bremner under control. The company was appearing week after week in the business pages and Low and Kelly worked closely together during that period.

One thing Dempsey could not be for anybody was a 'Yes' man. In public he measured his words carefully. His father had always taught him not to sink to the level of his opponents. If you did that you had lost the argument. In private, though, he could be blunt and colourful. 'There are different ways of motivating people,' he said. 'That's what management is all about'.

In the offices of SL Homes he could have a thoroughgoing four-lettered row with colleagues if he felt it was necessary and, once a decision had been reached, carry on as before, no grudges borne or resentments nursed. He brought the same approach to the plush Celtic boardroom with its light wood table and its view of the rich haul of football trophies from down the years, all too few of them from recent years. Until his arrival the meetings had been 'staid and indecisive', without any dynamism. The directors 'talked for hours'.

There was little attempt to deal with the real problems of the football world, let alone tackle the challenges of the 21st century. Dempsey accused them of incompetence in terms that would be understood on the terraces. 'I knew that with *The Taylor Report*, with Rangers building their commercial side and the way things were going generally, they needed help,' he said, 'but they also needed a bit of guts.'

Soon after Dempsey joined the Celtic board, the builder and property developer was approached by an Aberdeen-based property company called Jaymarke, which owned 430 acres of the former Robroyston Estate on the edge of Glasgow. They wanted to develop the land for housing. It had no planning permission, but they were confident they would get it. If Celtic successfully applied to build a stadium there, however, there was no doubt they would get permission for housing. But Jaymarke were a company in a hurry. Dempsey agreed to put up the money and keep the option open for Celtic.

Jaymarke and Dempsey's company Strathvale Holdings formed a new company called Bernlaw, to be 75 per cent owned by Jaymarke and 25 per cent by Strathvale, and each put money into the new company in the form of interest-free loans. Bernlaw then bought the land from Jaymarke for £2.5 million.

Under a supplementary agreement, Celtic had the right to buy Strathvale's share of the new company. They would buy the shares at the same nominal price that Strathvale had paid for them and repay Strathvale's loan. In return they would be *given* 40 acres of the land on which to build a stadium, with Jaymarke as the managing developer. The only other cost would be to upgrade a link road on the land from single to dual carriageway if the planning authorities insisted on it. In short: they would pay Dempsey's company back the £1.25 million it had cost him to keep the deal alive for them – and they would receive 40 acres of land plus a 25 per cent stake in the joint venture.

Most of Celtic's directors were enthusiastic about the idea. Company secretary Chris White and the newly arrived Michael Kelly were against it. They said it was too risky. Dempsey, as a Celtic supporter and because of his own nature, was anxious to prove that he would be good for Celtic. 'If it doesn't come off, I'll take the land back,' he told the board.

The reason hinted at in subsequent months of Dempsey's removal was that he was trying to line his own pockets with his plan for Robroyston. Journalists would be told there was more hehind his removal than could be revealed for 'obvious' legal reasons. Many of the same journalists and others, including the authors, were invited by Dempsey to read the contracts. The veiled accusations made against him did not appear in print.

In bound form, the contracts and letters of agreement concerned with Robroyston, still kept in the offices of SL Homes, are literally three-quarters of an inch thick, but their wording is quite clear. Clause 2.2 of the agreement concerning Celtic says: 'The price to be payable for the shares shall be the subscription price paid by Strathvale . . .' In other words, Dempsey would make nothing on their sale.

Clause 2.3 says: 'For the avoidance of doubt Strathvale shall have no claim or interest of any nature whatsoever under or arising from the terms of the Development Agreement . . .' Clause 2.6 says: 'For the avoidance of doubt . . . Strathvale shall have no further interest of any nature whatsoever in the company . . .' in other words, Dempsey's company would not be involved any more. And the contract spells out what the land was to be used for: ' . . . the development and construction of a modern football stadium primarily for use by Celtic with a seating capacity of 55,000 to 60,000 incorporating all necessary parking, premises for ticket sales, food sales, beverage sales and memorabilia sales . . .'

Dempsey did make a profit on Robroyston. When Celtic failed to take up their rights, he stayed in the deal and made money that Celtic could have had. Later he would say: 'All it needed was a bit of vision and a bit of guts.' He had kept money tied up in the land, trying to hold the deal open while Celtic directors made up their minds. 'We ran our business £1.25 million short during a recession because of them.'

One day, after a meeting to discuss Bremner, Kelly told Low that Dempsey was 'not a real Celtic man'. There were other comments over the weeks. Low became convinced Dempsey was going to be removed from the board before he war really on iy. Kelly's comments to Low about Dempsey became more frequent.

After the season ended, Billy McNeill had a form of revenge on Aberdeen when he signed the out-of-contract Charlie Nicholas from them for £450,000, bringing the international striker back to Parkhead after an absence of seven years. Nicholas was in time for a summer tour of friendly games in Germany and Holland which included a 6-0 win over the German side TSV Ottersberg. But a month later Celtic were struggling against part-timers Queen of the South who were fresh from knocking Dundee and Dunfermline out of the Skol Cup. It was nine minutes from time before substitute Joe Miller scored his team's second goal to put the Dumfries visitors out.

They went on to knock out Dundee United in the semi-final, though they could manage only to draw against them at Parkhead a week before the final. But for the board there was the consolation of a healthy 34,363 attendance. With a cup final imminent – and against Rangers, too – there was no reason to expect any fall-out at the annual general meeting two days before.

When the blow fell, the surprise of fans and the media at Dempsey's removal was matched only by the shock at the way in which it was done. Annual general meetings of the club had always been small, cosy private affairs. Sometimes they had trouble making up a quorum and the usual number of shareholders was around a dozen. The manager would be invited to make a little speech. Discussions ranged only as far as how well the manager was doing, what players he should buy, the quality of pies and whether they should change the supplier.

Corporate intrigue had been absent from the club for decades and the AGM called for 26 October 1990 was ostensibly to confirm routine business: to re-elect directors retiring by rotation, approve the accounts, set the directors' remuneration and re-appoint the auditors. As Kelly and Dempsey had been co-opted by the board, they had to be approved by the shareholders. Dempsey had 'flu that night and felt awful, but there was never any dount he would make the meeting.

As usual before an AGM the directors sat down to dinner in the Walfrid Restaurant, named after the man whose Poor Children's Dinner Table had once been supported from Celtic's profits. Usually the only business discussed was who would propose and second the resolutions due to be put to the shareholders. The meal lasted about an hour and a quarter but neither White nor Kelly warned Dempsey of what they would do. Then just before they went to the Jock Stein Lounge where the shareholders were gathering, Michael Kelly told him his confirmation as a director was going to be opposed.

In spite of his shock at this casual announcement, Dempsey recovered his composure enough to say: 'There's no need to do this.' He was an experienced businessman, he knew how things were done. If they didn't want him all they had to do was say so quietly. He would wait until the season was over to avoid a bublic row which might affect the team, then resign and blame pressure of work. Financially he had nothing to lose. The director's fees never rose above £2,500 for a full year. But the memory that is burned into Dempsey's mind is of Michael Kelly saying: 'We need to do it.'

The shareholders meeting began with the routine business of every annual general meeting. The minutes of the previous AGM were read, approved and signed by the Chairman. The directors' report and accounts were approved unanimously – after a question about the catering facilities. The director's fees were fixed at the existing level of £2,500 a year. There was, as usual, not so much as a vote by a show of hands. The resolutions were proposed, seconded and went through without dissent. This had always been the Celtic way.

Kevin Kelly was re-elected as a director, unanimously. Tom Grant was re-elected as a director, unanimously. Michael Kelly's co-option was put to the meeting for confirmation. It was approved, unanimously.

Dempsey's co-option was put to the meeting for confirmation. White objected. For the first time, a resolution went to a show of hands. There were 34 shareholders either present or represented by proxies. His appointment was approved 17 to 13, with a majority of the directors, including the Chairman, voting for him.

White then called for a poll vote in accordance with Article 54 of the club's constitution. At first no one showed any sign of knowing what he meant. A show of hands was rare enough, but a vote based on the number of shares rather than the number of shareholders present was unheard of. But as he had shares or proxies amounting to ten per cent or more of the club he was entitled to call for such a vote.

The auditors, Hardie Caldwell, handed out voting slips. When the result was read out, Dempsey's co-option had been defeated by 733 votes to 472 with 20 abstentions. McGinn thanked Dempsey for his efforts on behalf of the club in the short time he had been a director and wished him well for the future. Dempsey thanked the Chairman for the courtesy and help given to him while he had been a director, wished the club and the board well for the future and said he left with no ill-will towards anybody. It was a dignified performance.

Inside he felt hurt and betrayed. 'I felt worse because the other four did not stand beside me. There wasn't really a lot of courage about. I felt let down.'

Michael Kelly told the meeting they must now look to the future and the complex issues ahead, including whether they redeveloped Parkhead or moved to a new site. Yet Kelly, White and their supporters had just closed one option for the club. Kelly later told Dempsey it had been White's idea.

Farrell went to Dempsey after the vote and suggested a cup of tea. 'You might try to put some artificial dignity on this,' said Dempsey. 'I don't have to.' Weak with 'flu and deep disappointment, he left Parkhead to make a lonely journey home to Fairways, Milngavie, to the north-west of the city.

Immediately after the AGM four directors, including Kevin Kelly, met to discuss what Farrell later called 'the dirty deal over Brian Dempsey' and their dissatisfaction with the attitude of Michael Kelly and Chris White. The team, training at Seamill, saw the news reports of the 'dirty deal'. Dempsey, who received phone calls from well-wishers all the next day, refused to start a slanging match in spite of being given a perfect opportunity by the *Sunday Mail*. He went along to Hampden and shouted as much as his 'flu would let him, but it could not stop Celtic losing 2-1.

Chapter Three

THE FIRST DEAL

I

DEMPSEY went back to his business. In spite of his 'flu he had to turn up at his office to show people he was not shirking anything , then he took his family to Ireland. Other than a brief interview in the *Sunday Mail* in which he expressed surprise at his removal, he maintained his silence for nearly four months. Subsequent announcements from Parkhead, though, prompted him to speak out publicly.

Some executive box holders and Executive Club members wanted to mount a boycott. The executive boxes, high up beneath the roof of the stand, cost £25,000 a year. Executive Club members paid an annual subscription of £470 for a reserved centre stand seat with drinks before and after the game. But one of the conditions of Executive Club Membership was that you had to lend Celtic £2,000 free of interest. And if you paid up your loan over 12 months you had to pay £2,100, which meant you gave Celtic an interest-free loan and if you did not pay it all at once, Celtic effectively charged you five per cent interest on your loan to them. But Celtic had to repay these loans if the member chose to quit the club. Dempsey spoke out against a boycott and kept on his own three executive boxes. However, leaks about a board divided over the stadium issue continued.

Back at Bremner, Low asked Kelly what was going on. Kelly only hinted at doubts about the Robroyston plan. Not knowing what lay ahead, Low said: 'I have a feeling this could come back to haunt you, Michael. You have set a precedent for how future affairs will be handled. This is my field. I hope you know what you are doing.'

Now he was interested. From Companies House he obtained the accounts of Celtic and all its associated companies as far back as 1982 and studied them. His conclusion was that there were major problems ahead for the club. Football had started to change in the mid-1980s and the key point for Celtic was when Lawrence Marlborough took over Rangers. He removed the old guard. He brought in David Holmes as chief executive and gave him a large budget. Souness arrived, who brought in Terry Butcher and other international stars. The stakes in Scottish football had been raised substantially.

From 1986 to 1988 Celtic did not pay any attention. Then Rangers ran into financial difficulties. David Murray bought the club and started spending even more money. Celtic's old guard, Desmond White and Tom Devlin, had gone but the young guard's only response was to start imitating Rangers. The club began going into debt. In 1986 the overdraft was only £15,000. Rangers' borrowings mounted too, but they were able to manage their debt. Celtic lacked the expertise.

Low spent a month, on and off, analysing the figures. There was a trend. The club was in trouble. The majority of the board had recognised it and brought in Dempsey but they were blocked by White and Kelly. Celtic in its present form could not continue. He did not know what the changes would be or how they would manifest themselves but Celtic Football Club was entering a new era.

He did not know Dempsey at this stage and had no reason to doubt Kelly. After all, Kelly was a former Lord Provost, a Justice of the Peace, an eminently respectable figure by any standards. Low even wrote a letter to *The Herald* supporting Kelly and White on the basis of what he had been told.

When Low became Chairman of Bremner, it brought another Celtic connection into play. Carswell, the stockbroking firm still owned by Bremner, had employed Sir Robert Kelly, Celtic's Chairman for 24 years until just before

49

his death in 1971, and referred to in the Press as Mr Celtic. Sir Robert's Celtic connections had brought a lot of business to Carswell and the Celtic relationship continued after he left.

As Chairman of Carswell, Low came across a letter early in 1991 from a James G. Kelly of Oceanside, California. He was the son of a cousin of Michael Kelly who had emigrated and they had lost touch. James G. – known as Graham – Kelly wanted to sell his 'interest in the Glasgow Celtic football organisation' and as the club was not listed on the Stock Exchange his father had suggested Carswell could arrange a private sale. If a buyer could be found 'willing to pay a fair price' he wanted Carswell to sell at their discretion.

Graham's 'interest in the Glasgow Celtic football organisation' amounted to 120 partly-paid shares. Carswell wrote back that they had notified a number of people that the shares were for sale, including Celtic's board, but the sale would have to be handled by another firm of brokers, BWD Rensburg. Low was shutting down Carswell as part of his plan to transform Bremner. There was another reason: he himself wanted the shares and Carswell could not handle the sale without a conflict of interest.

Rensburg offered the shares to the board, to Brian Dempsey, his business partner John Keane and Michael Kelly, among others, without revealing the seller's identity. The board put a value on the shares of only £3 each. Yet when Tom Devlin had died in 1986, his executors had had his shares valued and £3 was the price placed on them then. Low decided to have the shares valued independently by accountants Rutherford, Manson & Dowds. They put a value on them of £59.56 each – nearly 20 times the value set by the board. Instead of the board's value of £360 for all Graham's shares, Low offered £12,000, or $24,000. Graham Kelly was delighted, but the board were not. They did not want to buy the shares, certainly not at that price.

Michael Kelly, whose firm was still retained by Bremner, called Low. After some general conversation he asked about the shares. Low told him it was his cousin selling them. Kelly said he wanted to keep the shares in the family because they had been his grandfather's. He rang Graham in California and told him the same. He let his cousin know that the board could block the transfer of the shares. Under the Articles of Association – or constitution – of The Celtic Football and Athletic Company Ltd, the board had the right to block the transfer of shares to anybody of whom they disapproved. The implication was that no one else could buy the shares. Meanwhile he tried to find out who was bidding for them. His big fear was that Dempsey would buy them.

Kelly would not bid the kind of money Low had offered so he encouraged Low. He wanted the shares in friendly hands and at that stage Low was not an opponent. Low asked if the board would register the transfer of shares and Kelly agreed to do his best to convince them they should. Low increased his bid to nearly £20,000, or $40,000, conditional on the board ratifying the transfer. In the end, though, they went to John Keane for an unconditional bid of around £20,000, more than £160 each . . . and more than 50 times the value placed on them by the board.

From this point on, Low began to view Kelly in a different light. But something more important had taken place: the first share deal in the takeover battle, the start of the rebels' share accumulation, the point at which the rebellion began.

II

'CHIEF EXECUTIVE, Celtic Football club, £60k, bonus, car, etc,' read the advert. 'Football is no longer just a Saturday afternoon! The public's leisure requirements, sponsors' demands, international opportunities and legislation such as *The Taylor Report*, all require increasing sophistication and enforce continued change which cannot be financed from just ticket revenue.'

The new man would have a big job to do: 'The Chief Executive will be responsible for ensuring the long-term profitability of the club, the provision of a 21st-century stadium and for providing the infrastructure to support and finance the team in whichever direction European and world football moves.'

And the man they wanted? 'Probably at least 40, your career will clearly demonstrate success in general management of large-scale, fast-moving, market-led organisations, with experience of managing multi-million pound projects an advantage.'

The club needed an executive who could bring order to a company which operated without pre-set budgets or tight financial controls. Until June 1990 the club's accounts were kept by Desmond White, Arkbuckle & Co and although they satisfied the minimum requirements of the Companies Act they contained too little information for modern management accounting. A computerised accounting system was introduced only that year.

Not all the board were convinced Terry Cassidy was the man they wanted, even if he once spent six months as a teenage professional footballer in Nottingham. His selection had the support of only four of the six directors, although when it was announced it was put out as the unanimous decision of the board. He was 53 and had been chief executive of Outram's, predecessor of Caledonian Newspapers which publish *The Herald* and *Evening Times*, yet it came to seem he had learned little about handling the Press. His contract was to run for three years from 1 January 1991 at £75,000 a year, with the option of being renewed for periods of 18 months, and with a bonus and salary review at the end of each year.

He had a reputation for being unnecessarily abrasive. Jimmy Farrell later called him 'the master of the gratuitous insult'. At one point Tom Grant was reduced almost to tears and offered his resignation because he felt Cassidy was destroying Celtic's reputation in the Press. He felt so strongly that he had to be 'brow-beaten' by Farrell and others into withdrawing it.

In his first month Cassidy announced that he had to be convinced that Brian Dempsey was interested in Celtic's 'good health'. A meeting with Dempsey failed to smooth their relationship. Dempsey blames that and other Cassidy remarks for the breaking of his silence. Cassidy was soon giving interviews explaining the myriad of options open to him. He had received 11 proposals for proposed stadia, including one to build a stadium at no cost to the club, 'in addition to the Robroyston option', and obtaining the finance was 'no problem'.

Yet the club's debts were already £3 million and the team had won only seven of their last 22 league matches, were 18 points behind Rangers and were out of Europe. Enough supporters were concerned to launch the first of the pressure groups trying to reverse the club's fortunes, Save Our Celts, founded by Willie Wilson. They held their inaugural meeting at Shettleston Halls on a February Sunday and attracted a crowd of 500 for a three-hour rally. Their intention was to set up an independent supporters association 'with direct access to the board'.

Cassidy was in the United States. Michael Kelly and Chris White had been invited but did not attend, although Tom Grant and Jimmy Farrell, sat at the top table. The West of Scotland's best-known criminal lawyer, Joe Beltrami, agreed to chair the meeting. A former Lisbon Lion, Jim Craig, spoke but the star of the show, applauded and cheered by the fans, was Brian Dempsey. He told the board, 'Stop the paranoia that if anyone dares to ask a question, he is creating mischief. We are not.'

The financial position worsened with an acrimonious dispute between Cassidy and Celtic's shirt sponsor, the Dumfermline-based double-glazing firm C.R. Smith. The firm's owner Gerard Eadie, spent £300,000 on the sponsorship and another £100,000 through his executive box at Parkhead. Typically the club claimed it had four major companies ready to spend more in sponsorship but a year later Cassidy was explaining why he had just turned down only £130,000 from another sponsor and, anyway, they were better off without a shirt sponsor – they would get more from sales of Celtic strips without one. Cassidy's dispute with Eadie meant that £116,000 of the shirt sponsorship for 1990-1991 was not received and the outstanding amount was cancelled during negotiations in 1993 for sponsorship from . . . C.R. Smith. By then the club were happy to take substantially less than Cassidy had initially rejected.

At the time, however, the chief executive was hinting heavily at an £11 million sportswear deal. Even before it was announced he was saying that with proper marketing they might double that £11 million. The deal was not announced until eight months later. It was worth £9.4 million in guaranteed payments over eight years, with bonuses based on performance and on sales. Sportswear firm Umbro forecast bonuses of around £2 million over the eight years, but no method of monitoring sales was negotiated.

Slipping consistently behind Rangers had a morale-sapping effect on supporters and players. Celtic captain Paul McStay began thinking what for him was the unthinkable – leaving the club after more than ten years. That season Celtic had failed to beat Rangers once in their first four encounters, managing at best a 1-1 draw. That was followed by 1-2 and 2-0 defeats in the league and a 2-1 disappointment in the Skol Cup final.

When they met again in a televised quarter final of the Scottish Cup at Parkhead, both sides were hungry for victory: Rangers because the Cup had eluded them for ten years in spite of their success elsewhere; Celtic to take away the bitter taste of three consecutive Old Firm defeats and to keep alive hopes of their first trophy for two years. The score, measured in goals, was a decisive 2-0 to Celtic, thanks to Gerry Creaney and Dasiusz Wdowczyk. But the score could also be measured in four red cards and seven other bookings. McNeill praised both the performance and the restraint of his side. Souness apologised for his. 'I would never had thought they were capable of that,' he said, and added that the Celts were 'worthy winners'.

Rangers had Terry Hurlock and Mark Walters sent off, both for elbowing Tommy Coyne at different times, followed by Mark Hately, already booked, for a reckless lunge at Anton Rogan. The fact they were all English perhaps proved that the seriousness of the match was no mere local feeling. The mood of the 50,837 crowd was tense and police lined the trackside at the Rangers end throughout the second half.

Celtic lost Peter Grant after he was first booked for pulling Mo Johnston's shirt only seconds before charging out of the wall as Ian Ferguson took a free kick. An Ian Ferguson free kick could have cost Celtic Paul Elliott after it hit him full in the face, but he coolly came off to change his bloodied shirt and went back to win the Man of the Match award. Elliott had been asking for a transfer not so much because of a contractual dispute as the way it was handled with 'very little communication between the club and me'.

Communication was proving to be another of the club's weak points.

III

PACKY BONNER – that great rarity in football, a one-club man – was looking forward to an enormous turn-out for his testimonial match against the Republic of Ireland on 12 May 1991. But the talking point of the weekend changed when *The Sun* revealed the existence of a memo from Terry Cassidy to the board outlining the best way to deal with the dismissal of manager Billy McNeill.

As part of probably the longest partnership between a captain and a manager, Jock Stein, McNeill was already a Celtic legend. The second most league appearances for Celtic, nine championship medals, seven Scottish Cup medals, six League Cup medals, two European Cup finals and, most memorably of all, one European Cup victory, he was the leader of the pride of lions at Lisbon. His second incarnation at Parkhead was as the manager who took over from Stein but his five-year term ended when the board refused to give him a written contract or a salary that matched his performance and position. McNeill went south to manage Manchester City and later Aston Villa but after four years he was invited back, complete with contract and salary. Now, after another four years later, he was about to be removed in the most premeditated way. Cassidy's memo not only laid out the sequence of meetings to be followed but even included a draft Press release announcing that assistant manager Tommy Craig had been offered the post of caretaker manager.

Cassidy at first said he did not know of any such papers but two days later – during which he had sat next to McNeill during Bonner's testimonial match – he admitted writing the memo as a guidance note for the board. In the meantime McNeill had guaranteed Celtic a place in Europe with a 3-2 win over St Johnstone on the Saturday.

The crowd showed much more Celtic spirit than their chief executive at Bonner's testimonial against a Republic of Ireland side, with 38,675 of them packing into Parkhead to contribute £250,000 to his testimonial year. Having both teams playing in green, with only the white hoops differentiating Celtic, summed up the mood for the day. Packy had brought over more than 50 relations and the fans in the Jungle stayed behind after the game to cheer him. In that emotional atmosphere it was forgivable to let in two goals, but Gerry Creaney preserved the hosts' honour with a hat-trick.

But there was little honour in the way McNeill was treated and for the second time as manager the manner of his departure two weeks later was unworthy of Celtic. The manner of replacing him reflected little credit on the club, either, with the decision process becoming drawn out. The very public short-list consisted of assistant manager Tommy Craig, former Irish internationals Liam Brady and Frank Stapleton, and former Yugoslav international Ivan Golac. They trooped up to meet the Parkhead board in turn.

It was Brady who was given the task of facing his new opposite number at Rangers. Walter Smith had taken over after the surprise departure of Graeme Souness for Liverpool. The Old Firm became the New Firm and the coming season held a promise of fresh excitement.

There was concern, too, after a tour of Brady's native Ireland resulted in a 2-0 defeat by Cork, a 0-0 draw against Dundalk and four injuries. But there was reassurance when Brady took his Boys, followed by 12,000 Celtic supporters, to his old playing haunt of Highbury for a testimonial match against Arsenal. Another Arsenal old boy, Charlie Nicholas, opened the scoring in a ding-dong game that rewarded both sides with two goals.

But in 1991 the overdraft soared from £2.9 million to more than £5 million after Brady went shopping for new players, among them the £1 million Tony Cascarino from Aston Villa, the £295,000 Gary Gillespie from Liverpool and goalkeeper Gordon Marshall who cost £270,000 from Falkirk. There was friction with Cassidy, including a memo from him about backroom staff salaries, and after the season had started there were newspaper adverts for executive boxes at 'great last-minute savings'.

The season started well with plenty of goals in a 3-4 win over Dundee United and a 3-1 dispatching of Raith Rovers, but before long familiar complaints and matching results returned. If anything, things were worse. By mid-September they had failed in five out of six games which included a 0-2 defeat at the hands of Rangers, and they had been humiliated in the Skol Cup by Airdrie. Then they found some form. An away draw against Antwerp's Germinal Ekeren put them into the second round of the UEFA Cup with a 1-3 win on aggregate. They dealt Hearts a 3-1 defeat at Parkhead and Tommy Coyne and Charlie Nicholas took turns to give Motherwell a sample of the recovery at Fir Park.

Low saw little of the decline or the comeback. He had been preoccupied with taking Bremner back to the Stock Market and dealing with 16 law suits outstanding from the boardroom battle. He was also helping to set up a recording studio in Glasgow with Allan McNeill, the manager of Scottish rock duo, Hue & Cry. He was planning to move his home and business from Edinburgh to Glasgow, his wife, Noelle, was expecting their third child. It took another incident to bring him into the centre of the Celtic story: a meeting with Brian Dempsey. It was a journalist who provided the connection.

One of the first journalists to cover the Bremner saga was Francis Shennan, then with *The Sunday Times* in Glasgow. In spite of a grandfather who was Chairman of Liverpool Schools Football Association, Shennan's interest in football was purely journalistic. He had led a *Sunday Times Scotland* investigation into the lack of emergency medical cover at many Scottish football grounds in the wake of the Hillsborough disaster. When he became the paper's Scottish Business Editor, he commissioned the first Price Waterhouse report into the financial state of Scottish football.

At the time football finance was little reported. The team at Price Waterhouse, led by partner Ian Dewar, reached a stunning conclusion. A third of Scotland's senior clubs would be insolvent but for the increased value given to their grounds in the accounts. It was almost unbelievable and there were those who did not believe it. After weeks of work, *The Sunday Times* did not run the story. Shennan was left to have it published in a football magazine called *The Punter*.

Among other football finance stories Shennan covered the takeover battle between Hearts and Hibs and the quixotic attempt of a group of Irish businessmen to launch a Dublin City Football Club into the Scottish Football League, in both of which Low was employed as a consultant. In the face of ridicule from traditional sports journalists, they found their views coincided on the future of football, the changes needed in a new era, and the importance of a skilled, professional approach in the boardroom to match the skills and professionalism on the field. For a brief period they formed a company called ClairVision, which attempted to become a documentary script development company, and their research and predictions for Scottish football eventually appeared in *CA*, a leading Scottish business magazine.

While researching a non-football story Shennan was introduced to a surveying consultant, Tom Brennan, who was planning a conference for surveyors on the leisure industry. Shennan mentioned the report on football finance and the role of ground revaluations, and suggested Low as a speaker at the conference. Brennan's office was in a building belonging to Brian Dempsey, who was also due to chair the conference.

On 9 October 1991 Dempsey and Low met at his office, then in South Street, Glasgow, ostensibly to talk about the conference. In reality, Low wanted to size up Dempsey. He knew there was something wrong with Celtic. He had heard the Kelly version. He had seen at first hand how Kelly and the board had reacted over Graham Kelly's shares. Now he had a chance to hear the other side.

Dempsey showed Low all the plans for Robroyston and the deal he had proposed. It added up. It made sense. The cynical, analytical Low could not fault it. He gave Dempsey his financial analysis. They agreed Celtic were on a slippery slope to nowhere. Low decided Dempsey had been removed because he was a threat to the established order, to the dynasty of Whites and Kellys. Dempsey represented the new era in football that Celtic had to be a part of to survive. The dynasty was part of the former era.

In the next few weeks Dempsey and Low met once or twice a week. They agreed something should be done, but what? The ruling families commanded a majority of the shareholding. Through the board they had a veto on the transfer of shares. The accepted belief was that Celtic was immune from takeover. Dempsey was concerned, too, that if they moved against the board he would be regarded as acting for the wrong reasons, from a desire for revenge.

Low had just emerged victorious from a battle to unseat two warring fractions who had taken a company to the brink of disaster. The lessons were still fresh in his mind. He suggested starting the same way he had at Bremner. They would begin by gathering the support of the shareholders. If the shareholders were not interested in supporting them, they would offer to buy the shares. The board could refuse to register the shares, but the rebels would not only buy the shares they would insist on the seller signing a proxy agreement which could not be revoked. That would transfer the votes of the shareholder to the rebels and the board could not block it.

When they had enough support they would demand seats on the board. The demand would be turned down, at which point they would exercise their right as representatives of more than ten per cent of the company to demand an extraordinary general meeting where the rebels would be voted on to the board. Once on the board, they would use their enormous support to remove the dynasties from power and begin revitalising the club.

The weapons in the war would be shareholder lists, proxy agreements, company law, contracts, meetings and money. The army would be shareholders and supporters, people who had been forgotten or ignored, punters whose views were not taken seriously enough. The campaign would take two years. It was now October 1991. The last EGM, which the board narrowly won, followed two years and one month afterwards in November 1993. That was the board's fatal victory. That was when the defences began crumbling until they finally toppled 14 weeks later.

Chapter Four

THE PRINCE

I have been questioning repeatedly, at board meetings, of our secretary whether or not this club is solvent and I have been told that the bank has not bothered us so we must be solvent.

— Jimmy Farrell to shareholders on events in 1991

I

THE new-found form under Liam Brady continued with a 4-1 thrashing of Dundee United, a display which was launched with two first-half goals from Charlie Nicholas. It pushed Celtic's unbeaten run to seven games but that was as far as it got. They had to fight back from being 1-3 behind at half-time against Falkirk to finish 'only' 3-4 down but could do nothing in the second-round UEFA Cup-tie with the Swiss team Neuchatel Xamas who hammered them 5-1. 'We were lucky it was only 5-1,' said Brady of the 'shambles'. Still they managed the footballing equivalent of kicking the cat by returning to thrash St Mirren 0-5 and putting Aberdeen in their place 2 -1 at Parkhead.

Off the field, too, it was a period of similar false dawns. Cassidy had hoped to agree a sportswear deal which would have Gola as combined kit and shirt sponsor. Instead, he managed to agree a deal with the existing kit sponsor

Umbro, hailed as a record kit deal. But the first year's payments, which were not due for another year anyway, were more than swallowed up by Brady, whose sale of Paul Elliott, Lex Baillie and Alex Mathie had not balanced his transfer books, paying Middlesbrough £1 million for Tony Mowbray.

A month later Cassidy promised a meeting of the Independent Celtic Supporters Association that Celtic would have the best stadium in Europe by 1994. At the same meeting was Celtic fan and former university business studies lecturer, Professor Tom Carberry. He summed up of Cassidy's chances of finding £45-£50 million for a new stadium as: 'If he can do this, he's Houdini.'

What he did not know was that just after the start of that season the Bank had already expressed concern about Celtic's financial state. 'In September and October 1991 the bank wrote to us and told us we would need to recapitalise,' Jimmy Farrell told shareholders months later. The Bank wanted the board to issue new shares to bring in more money. The number of shares in Celtic Football Club – 20,000 shares of £1 each – had not been increased since 1919. This meant that a share capital of £20,000 had to support a debt of £5 million. The directors asked the club's lawyers, McGrigor Donald, to look at the situation.

Farrell consulted Celtic financial manager Peter Lawell and asked him, point blank, if the club were solvent. 'If you take into consideration the transfer market of the players, yes,' said Lawell. 'If you don't do that you are not solvent.'

Only two clubs in Britain – Tottenham Hotspur and Hearts – had included players in the balance sheets. The inclusion had to be noted in the accounts because accountants held diametrically opposing views on whether or not it should be done. The view shared by Spurs and Hearts was that is was nonsense to exclude the club's biggest investment after the ground itself. If you could include the company cars in the balance sheet and work out the depreciation in their value, you could do the same with players.

On the other side were accountants who believed that players were too unpredictable – too human, in fact – to be treated that way. An injury, a sudden loss of form, a disillusionment with the game or with the club, could send a player's value plummeting. You could insure the company cars against damage, but the cost of insuring a player against injury was far higher, and you could not insure against a loss of form, that indefinable magic that gives a player his worth.

On 6 December 1991 the directors met Kevin Sweeney, one of the senior corporate finance partners at McGrigor Donald. Sweeney, a member of the Dunn family who own Joseph Dunn, bottlers of the popular Solripe lemonade and other fizzy drinks, was in his early fifties, ruddy-faced beneath his greying hair. His appearance was in sharp contrast to that of his colleague, Elspeth Campbell, a cool blonde in her early thirties.

The law firm occupied several of the half-dozen floors of Pacific House, a modern glass and stone building in Wellington Street, in Glasgow's city centre. Sweeney read them his conclusions: 'On examination of the balance sheet we were immediately and predictably struck by the low level of capital base from which the company operates. Our second reaction was the balance sheet was completely underpinned by the development fund reserve and the absence of which would show a considerable deficit.'

In other words, Celtic needed this reserve not just for development, which is what it had been intended for, but to stop sinking further into debt. The reserve was actually a donation to the club by the Celtic Development Fund to which the supporters contributed. It was arguable that Celtic had no real right to it in legal terms. Without the annual contribution from the Development Fund the financial situation would have been critical.

'Each director would require to consider his own personal position in relation to the insolvency legislation and, in particular, to those provisions which deal with wrongful trading.' In plain English, the situation was so bad the directors were being warned by their own lawyers that without the reserve fund to dip into they risked committing a criminal offence just by trying to stay in business. This was more than two years before they finally surrendered their control over the ailing club.

The lawyers went on to warn that fixed assets had been included in the balance sheet at a value that exceeded any amount that could be raised if they had to be sold. 'Overall it does not present a healthy picture and it is difficult to disagree with the comments made by the Bank.'

McGrigor Donald concentrated on whether or not it was advisable to increase the share capital by issuing more shares to existing shareholders rather than other methods of raising long-term funding, 'for example, the introduction of outside shareholders or the creation of debenture stock'. They accepted that other solutions to improve the financial position of the company 'like selling players' could not be considered. Their conclusion was: 'We consider it is imperative that the issued share capital be increased at the earliest opportunity. The position is serious enough for the directors to be required to contemplate future possibilities which up until now have been unthinkable *like the demise of the company or its acquisition by someone with access to huge funds . . .*' (authors' italics).

II

THE blueprint for the takeover of Celtic was to be a book written 480 years ago. Niccolo Machiavelli finished *The Prince* in 1514. It is the reputation of this book that gave us the word Machiavellian to describe devious or clever strategies. But more people know about the book than have read it. It was written to help statesmen provide governments that would last, and stability was prized highly in the uncertain Middle Ages. Copies of the book disappeared from Glasgow shops as Low bought them a dozen at a time to help the rebels understand what they were embarking upon. He had to buy a second copy for himself after his first fell apart from over-use.

His plan was, in effect, to bring about a takeover without making a bid. It rested upon gaining the support of smaller shareholders, those ordinary people who had largely inherited their shares from forebears and relatives who had given a great deal to the club. They now kept the shares, without receiving dividends, and were largely ignored by the directors. A takeover without a bid had two major advantages: first, it would not enrich the men now being blamed for the state of the club, and second, it was feasible.

It was the only way to defeat a board who could stop new shareholders being registered.

Almost the first problem in dealing with each shareholder approached was to convince him or her it could be done. Nearly everybody had the desire for change but nearly everybody thought Celtic was a closed shop. Most at some point told Low he was wasting his time: 'It isn't possible. The board and their families have got it sewn up. '

Dempsey, who had most reason to be circumspect about Low, had been quick to respond. When Low first met Dempsey he was still seen as being close to Michael Kelly and Dempsey was suspicious. Low had appeared as a financial analyst on a BBC Scotland programme, *Focal Point*, in which he had criticised Dempsey. After Low had examined the Robroyston plan, he apologised to Dempsey for misjudging him. 'I had lots of doubts,' said Dempsey. 'It took me a long time to trust him and I told him so.' The trust grew with every new event. 'He assessed everything 99 per cent accurately: who would do what,' said Dempsey. 'He was always dead on.'

From the start Low dreamed up jokey codenames for each of the main participants. Celtic was codenamed 'Shinty' and the campaign was 'Operation Shinty'. Chris White became 'Meanie', Michael Kelly 'Shifty', Jimmy Farrell 'Sleepy', and Tom Grant 'Jammy'.

Low had, by his own admission, an analytical, cynical and calculating mind. In the heat of a corporate battle, with its stress, with rumours flying around, it is easy to become confused. You cannot always see the way ahead. Low was able to stand back and say 'If we go down this route we win.' His plan became known among the inner circle of rebels as 'Route One to Goal'. The name came from an old BBC television sports quiz called *Quizball* in which football personalities could pick one, two or three answer 'routes' to points or goals.

Money for share purchases would be put up by Dempsey and John Keane. In two years, £500,000 would be spent. The new rebel alliance began with shareholders outside Scotland. There was a good chance they had been most neglected and the rebels' activities were less likely to alert the board. The first foray was to be in Belfast.

On 1 November 1991 Low and an accountant friend, Paul McNeill, of the firm Pannell Kerr Forster, whose family were shareholders, took the Loganair flight from Glasgow to Belfast Harbour airport. A family connection had put them in touch with a shareholder in the north of Ireland. They met at 10 a.m. in a solicitor's office in Ormeau Road, a nationalist area not far from the city centre. The shareholder had heard the Michael Kelly view of Brian Dempsey and had supported Kelly and White. Then she had heard nothing more from them. Now she heard the other side of the story. As a result, 247 shares changed hands. With the shares went an irrevocable mandate and proxies. It was the only way round the board's veto on share transfers.

The two visitors went for a coffee at the Europa Hotel, probably the most bombed hotel in the world. The deal had taken less than an hour, and now they had to wait for the flight back. Nervous about just wandering around Belfast but keen to see something of the city, they decided to take a taxi around the main sights. Outside they knocked on the window of one of the taxis waiting outside the hotel. The driver jumped. There had recently been a spate of kidnappings of taxi drivers. Low and McNeill offered the driver £50 to give them a tour of the city. They left the choice of landmarks to him.

He began predictably enough with Stormont but then he took in the Shankhill Road and Falls Road. Finally he took them to Milltown Cemetery and stopped. This was the graveyard where a Loyalist gunman had thrown hand grenades and opened fire on mourners at a Republican funeral. Nearby two British soldiers in plain clothes who had stumbled into another funeral had been stripped and beaten to death.

More than a little nervously they got out and followed the driver inside. The Republican graves had florid, Italianate statues on them. The taxi driver showed them around the graveyard the way a guide would show tourists round a castle: 'This is the grave of hunger striker Bobby Sands . . . across there is the grave of . . . and this is where . . .' For him the sights of Belfast included the graves of young men.

Their next stop was a Republican club in the Ardoyne, but by now it was difficult to refuse. They had to pass three different security barriers, all manned by Republicans, to get in. Low entered wearing a Celtic tie and badge. He had neither when he left. The customers of the club had all wanted souvenirs of Celtic.

III

FIVE days after returning from Ireland, Low phoned the father of James Graham Kelly in Las Vegas. They agreed in principle to the sale of his shares for $300 a share. The rebels had started their advance.

Brian Dempsey was very close to Betty Devlin, widow of the former Celtic Chairman Tom Devlin. He had already been with Celtic 36 years when he became Chairman in spite of his age and less than perfect health, but he had a clear idea of his and the directors' roles. He wanted to show the fans there was 'a team behind the team'. Mrs Devlin was quick to put her weight behind the rebels because she did not believe the current board were that kind of team. With 1,747 shares she was the largest shareholder in the club after Chris White. So, in less than a month, they could speak for ten per cent of the club.

On 18 November 1991, Low flew to Canada and met Fergus McCann for the first time. His task was to get the Scots-Canadian millionaire involved in the plan. McCann had a second-floor executive flat in the heart of Montreal's old quarter – old at least in Canadian terms. McCann, though, was Scottish, brought up in Kilsyth, a small, unprepossessing town about 15 miles out of Glasgow on the way to Stirling. Celtic director Jimmy Farrell called regularly to see McCann's father, Alan, a headmaster in Stirlingshire.

Fergus was always a Celtic fan and in his late teens was social convenor of the Celtic Supporters' Club which met at the miners' welfare hall in nearby Croy. He was an apprentice with a small Glasgow firm of accountants but at 22 he emigrated to Canada. There he worked in the marketing departments of major companies such as Seagrams and Pretty Polly. The twin disciplines of financial control and marketing were essential for good sports promotion and were irresistible when allied with firm ideas about what he wanted.

In the early 1970s he decided there was money in marketing Scottish golfing holidays, especially in the home of golf, St Andrews, to Canadians and Americans. He ignored the traditional tourism market and advertised in *Golf Digest*, an American monthly magazine with a circulation of two million. His holiday packages included everything, from meals to tee-off times. Every customer stayed on his files and was sold to again and again. To St Andrews he added trips to the British Open, Ireland and Bermuda, the tax haven where he moved his operations company. In 15 years he had sold the company for $8 million and concentrated on Firstgreen Ltd.

With Firstgreen, an investment company specialising in large-scale projects, there was a chance for heart and head to work together, a potent combination, and he approached Celtic in 1988. Long before *The Taylor Report* he suggested that the club increase its seating capacity from 9,000 to 24,000 and provide standing accommodation for 48,000 to give it a more viable business base on which to run the stadium. He would provide a £5 million loan at a low-interest rate and marketing in return for a percentage of the increased revenue that would be generated. The low rate of six per cent was closer to the Canadian interest rate than the UK one which was around 14 per cent at the time and it would have saved the club £600,000 a year in interest payments.

There were several meetings with the club but by the following year he felt he was getting nowhere. He wrote to the board offering to buy the shares of any holder wanting to sell – something suggested to him at the EGM four years later – at a price of around £120 each. By then he was after a 51 per cent stake and a chief executive's role. But the directors made it clear they would oppose any such offer and would block the transfer of any shares. In a last-ditch attempt to deal with the board in 1990 he came back to Scotland and met Chris White and accountant Francis McCrossan to find a way through the obstructions. His style was direct to the point of bluntness, a characteristic that might have its roots in youthful shyness but was honed by business dealings in North America: 'What do you want? How can I help you? What kind of deal can I make?'

But they did not want to know. The position of strength they thought they had led them to treat McCann with arrogance. He tried to put together support for change, and during 1990 he met both Dempsey and Weisfeld but without result. Dempsey liked him, saw in him a good, honest, decent man, but they 'battled from Day One'. McCann returned to Canada annoyed and frustrated.

When he met Low on his Canadian trip, the style was unchanged. The furnishings in McCann's apartment were modern and unfussy, reflecting the same approach. The meeting began in a very tense manner. McCann was suspicious. Low had worked with Michael Kelly on Bremner and at first some of the rebels assumed he was a Kelly man. 'Who are you, Mr Low?' asked McCann. 'Why are you here? Who are you representing?' But he did not do what Jack McGinn once accused him of doing, 'asking questions and answering them himself'.

Low put forward his plan which was, to paraphrase the slogan of the fans two years later, to support the shareholders and sack the board, at least some of them. McCann knew about business. 'That's a good plan, Mr Low.'

McCann, though, had his own plan. He wanted to form a public limited company, Celtic's Future plc, put several million pounds into it from himself, Dempsey and their supporters and have this company take over the club. Low was very wary of the idea because he did not believe it would work. If the board did not accept a takeover bid, they would probably block it and their legal team could probably stop it too. Perhaps as big a problem would be trying to persuade supporters to put money into a company other than Celtic itself.

Their meeting lasted all morning and continued over lunch in a French restaurant in Montreal. The two men agreed that they had a common objective but disagreed on the way forward.

From Montreal Low flew to Toronto to meet Jim Doherty. A large man in his late thirties, with a deep drawl that contrasted with McCann's clipped conciseness, he looked more like an ice-hockey player than either the yacht broker he was or the avid soccer fan he was to become. He was a second cousin of Celtic director Tom Grant. Felicia Grant, of

Terry Cassidy, Kevin Kelly and Gwyn Kennedy reveal Celtic's vision of a bright new future in Cambuslang (Picture: The Celtic View)

The old board in discussion, featuring Michael Kelly, Kevin Kelly, Tom Grant and David Smith (Picture: The Celtic View)

John Collins, a big-money buy from Hibs (*Picture:* The Celtic View)

Tom Boyd joining the Bhoys from Chelsea (*Picture:* The Celtic View)

Club captain Paul McStay did everything he could to concentrate players' minds on events on *the field* (Picture: The Celtic View)

Charlie Nicholas, as senior player, spoke out on behalf of team members
(*Picture:* The Celtic View)

Fergus McCann arrives at Celtic Park for the final showdown
(*Picture:* The Celtic View)

Hail, Hail, the Celts are here … Eager Celtic fans await the
announcement of a new era at Celtic Football Club
(*Picture:* The Celtic View)

The new Celtic supremo … Fergus McCann (Picture: The Celtic View)

An historic Press conference … Brian Dempsey holds centre stage while Kevin Kelly and Fergus McCann survey the room
(*Picture:* The Celtic View)

A welcome aboard to Gerald Weisfeld from Fergus McCann
(*Picture:* The Celtic View)

New kids on the block … Willie Haughey, Gerald Weisfeld, Michael
McDonald and Paul Waterston (*Picture:* The Celtic View)

Toomebridge in the north of Ireland, the mystery lady who many fans believed made the club immune from takeover, was, up to her death in 1972, Celtic's largest shareholder. She left 1,729 shares to Grant's father, James – which Tom inherited in 1985 – and the remainder to five relatives in Ireland and five in Canada. It was a matter of annoyance to these relatives that so many shares had been left to James Grant. Doherty could speak for the Canadian five.

He had inherited his shares from an aunt and he was the first generation of Canadian shareholder who had taken an active interest. He wanted to get involved. To him Celtic represented his heritage and a connection to his roots. He was bitter at what he saw as the board's neglect of the shareholders, especially the overseas ones. It was to be a feeling expressed time after time by the minority shareholders, most of them – like Doherty's older relatives – ordinary working people. Adding to this grievance was the time the board had taken to register the transfer of his shares. Notices of annual meetings would arrive up to two weeks after they took place and were often wrongly addressed in spite of several requests to Chris White to correct his mailing list. Even before he met Low, Doherty disliked the board. 'They treated us like mushrooms,' he said; that is, the board kept them in the dark and threw sh . . manure at them.

The night that Brian Dempsey was removed from the board Tom Grant, obviously upset, had phoned Jim's aunt in Toronto. Shortly afterwards Grant was in Canada and the two cousins met for the first time. They sat in a Toronto pub surrounded by Celtic supporters and discussed the turmoil at Parkhead. The television behind the bar was showing the devastation unleashed by Operation Desert Storm in the Iraqi-occupied Kuwait. From that point Doherty held meetings with his Canadian relatives and became their spokesman.

The following March Doherty visited Glasgow and met Dempsey to hear his story. The next day he met Chris White who told him Dempsey had had a financial interest in Robroyston. 'I didn't buy that,' said the Canadian. 'I had met Dempsey by then.'

On St Patrick's Day he watched Celtic play for the first time: the tense clash of the Old Firm with four players red-carded and a fistful of other bookings. More importantly the Celts won 2-0. 'It was my first game,' said the burly Canadian. 'I was so full of emotion I had to bite my bottom lip to hold the tears back.'

He was hooked, and he was more than willing to meet Low when he arrived eight months later. They met in the cocktail bar of Toronto's Intercontinental Hotel where Low explained how he came to be involved and the plan he had drawn up. He quickly established that Doherty did not want to sell, he wanted to support the rebels. The big Canadian spoke for 872 shares. Now the rebels had 14 per cent.

The day after Low's return from Canada, on 22 November, he attended the annual dinner of Glasgow University Celtic Supporters' Club. Already rumours were spreading that something was afoot. Matt McGlone, editor of the irreverent fanzine *Once A Tim*, intended to mention in his next issue that Low had been in Canada seeing shareholders. And Kevin McKenna, then a freelance sports writer, now sports editor of *Scotland on Sunday* wanted to write a story.

Low, who had been hoping to do nothing more than unwind and let his hair down at a boozy function, was concerned. He had never expected rumours to leak so soon. He managed to dissuade McGlone from mentioning the trip and persuaded McKenna the rumours were unfounded. Three days later he met Shennan and independent film producer, and Celtic supporter, Peter Broughan, for drinks near the St Clair recording studios. The meeting was to discuss the market for television documentary projects and ideas for programmes on business, including football finance in general. Shennan, as a partner in ClairVision, had been told some of the story in confidence and was pressing to be released from that obligation.

However, the rebels' embryonic alliance needed nurturing. Low visited Mrs Devlin at home in Trinity, Edinburgh, to introduce himself and to cement the support they already had. They were unusual allies: a corporate finance specialist steeped in investment management, and a proud lively woman in her seventies, widow of a Celtic Chairman, with a passion for the club.

Doherty flew back to Glasgow and the following morning he and Low left for Belfast. Their mission was to make contact with the Irish Grants, who held the other half of the portion of shares that had gone to Canada. Doherty was meeting them for the first time. He had built up the trip in his mind as an emotional homecoming but at first it looked set to prove a disappointment. They were met at the airport by Aiden Neeson, who had 172 shares but was the Irish equivalent of Doherty in that he could speak for the Irish shareholders.

The first meeting took place in a 'cold, damp little room' on the first floor of a hotel in Toomebridge. He ordered a Coke and that was what he got – no ice. They were mainly older generation shareholders there. Low began the talking, then Doherty joined in. 'They didn't say a peep. I didn't get a response. They didn't lift their heads from the table. After about five minutes I asked: "What do you people think?" One of the women there said: "I don't know anything about soccer. Let's have a meal."'

They went downstairs and continued talking, but now the ice was broken. Their feelings were the same: they had been ignored by the board, but they had no power and could not do anything. Low presented the case against the Kellys and the Whites, the problems facing the club, the plan to remove them . . . with the Grants' support. They gave it. Ten weeks into the campaign and the rebels now had 19 per cent of the shareholders behind them.

No holding was too small to pursue, though. When it came to the crunch, every share would count. Low's study of the Celtic share register showed a holding of just five shares in the name of a Belfast lawyer. With only half an hour to spare if they were to catch the flight back to Glasgow he started making calls on his mobile phone. Directory inquiries had only one name matching the one on the share register. He rang the number and asked to speak to the lawyer, to the great surprise of the woman answering. It was a launderette. The legal firm had shut down 15 years ago.

But this was Belfast, which had a grapevine to rival any village. The woman knew the old lawyer had moved to another firm. When Low rang there he learned the lawyer had retired a long time ago . . . but by the kind of chance no fiction writer would dare to invent, he had called into the office that day. The lawyer put Low in touch with Austin

Donaghue who now had the shares. He and Doherty began running through the city centre. A passer-by warned them to slow down: 'You could get shot like that.' They went up an alley past sandbag barricades towards Donaghue's office, but it seemed worth it. Low was promised the proxy votes to the five shares.

It was a short-lived victory. The next week he received a letter to say the shares had been registered wrongly: they in fact belonged to Tom Grant. So the net effect of their race through Belfast was to give Grant another five shares which would eventually be tied into the opposition.

At the airport Low suggested switching flights. They went to Edinburgh instead of Glasgow so that Doherty could be introduced to Mrs Devlin. It was important for the allies to know and trust each other. Personal contact was essential. It was a lesson the board would learn too late.

'It was a real honour meeting Betty Devlin,' said Doherty. 'Here was the Iron Lady of Celtic Football Club. She let me hold the European Cup winners' medal presented to her husband. She is a big lady in my eyes and always will be.'

Back in Glasgow that night they met Tom Grant at the Pond Hotel on Great Western Road. The two cousins were getting on well but Grant did not want to meet Low. Grant still wrongly regarded him as a Kelly man. Three hours later he had changed his mind and was on their side. With Grant's holding at that time of 1,729 shares, the rebels now had 28 per cent.

Meanwhile Dempsey was a client of Shaughnessy, Quigley & McColl, where Jimmy Farrell was senior partner, and Dempsey had a close working relationship with him. The firm's association with Celtic was a century old – it had handled the transformation of the club into a limited company in 1897. If Farrell's shares could be counted on, they had assembled an alliance of 32 per cent – nearly a third of all the Celtic shares – in just two months.

Chapter Five

PATSY'S BOYS AND A LISBON LION

The best player I ever saw. He was unexcelled as a dribbler and ball-worker, was always direct in his approach to goal, had a most uncanny gift of being able to change speed in a single stride, and no one then or since has had such perfect balance.
– Sir Robert Kelly on Patsy Gallagher (quoted in *The Glory & The Dream* by Tom Campbell and Pat Woods)

ANOTHER cosy Celtic tradition had been ended in October when Kevin Kelly replaced Jack McGinn as Chairman, the first time for many years that an active Chairman had stepped down. They were usually more than ready to retire completely when they stood down. Low believed Kevin Kelly was there to be a patsy. They were going to have a rough two years and the men on the board knew it. Kelly was put there to take the flak.

By December rumours of 'something happening' had reached the Glasgow branch of the Stock Exchange. The 'Smoker' is the Stock Exchange's annual dinner in the city and several members were asking about Celtic. The prospects for the rebels were looking good. They had the support of a substantial shareholding in the club and they had not begun to approach the really small shareholders yet. Low and Dempsey, who were now meeting twice a week, had made contact with a major potential investor, Fergus McCann. In good spirits Low successfully bid £3,000 for a football autographed by the Lisbon Lions in the Smoker's charity auction.

The circle was growing wider but as it did so there was the increased danger of a leak. Shennan had been given information on a strictly confidential basis but now he was pressing to run a story. Low was opposed to it. Any story could alert the board and spark the beginnings of a defence strategy. Then *Scotland on Sunday* football correspondent Kevin McCarra telephoned Low. McCarra had moved from an academic background to become a highly literate and intelligent football writer with good contacts in the game. At that point he had not met Low but he realised there was more to the story than just rumours. The plan could not be kept quiet indefinitely.

McCann had put Low in touch with his then legal adviser in Scotland, Magnus Swanson of Maclay Murray & Spens, and they met at 8.30am on 10 December in Low's West End home. Swanson was in his thirties and very able. Originally from Caithness, he happened to be a Celtic supporter. McCann had instructed Swanson to release all his papers. But other potential money men were being sounded out.

Next day Low met Billy Connolly's former manager, Frank Lynch. He had returned to Scotland from South Carolina where he had emigrated after selling some of Glasgow's once trendy pubs and clubs such as the Muscular Arms and Maestro's. He remained a fervent Celtic supporter and had once considered making an outright bid for the club. Low was a friend of his son, Ralph, who had gone with his father to the States and returned with a Harvard business degree. He was now working with the merchant bank, Lehman Brothers, in London. Ralph had also considered trying to do something about Celtic with his father.

That same day Jim Doherty flew into Glasgow to stay with Tom Grant for the Celtic AGM, to be held on Friday the 13th. This AGM was to show there was no going back to the cosy shareholders meetings of previous years. The tactics of Chris White and Michael Kelly at the last AGM had closed the door on the past forever.

Proxies, which authorise others to speak and vote on behalf of shareholders, have to be lodged 24 hours in advance. The directors, and especially White and Kelly, must have wondered what was going on. A large number of Low's friends were listed as proxies. In fact, at that stage most of them just wanted to attend a Celtic AGM and there was no great game-plan, although among them was accountant Paul McNeill who had been on the first share-buying expedition to Belfast. McNeill was there as a proxy for Dempsey. It had been decided during the regular morning strategy meetings that it would be better if he did not attend himself.

There was more than ususal interest in the AGM, with around 60 shareholders present or represented by proxies, nearly double the previous year's attendance. Kelly opened the meeting by welcoming everyone and invited White to read the minutes, which he did in a faltering voice. Kelly asked if there were any questions. 'Yes, I have some,' said Low.

This was almost unprecedented. Celtic AGMs did not have questions like this. Shareholders might ask about the team and the pies, but who ever asked questions about the minutes? Low's questions were about the poll vote to remove Dempsey. 'Was it true that everybody had a vote on a show of hands? And was it true that on a poll vote it was a vote for every ten shares?'

White confirmed it was true. Low did not comment. What he was after was any information to support the argument that Dempsey's removal was invalid or questionable. White's answer did not help, but any piece of information might prove useful in the future. The club's Articles of Association, or constitution, laid down that shareholders had one vote for every ten shares they held. So the show of hands which supported Dempsey had been wrongly counted, and the poll vote which removed him had apparently been legally correct, but an irregularity would come to light later.

White gave a summary of the accounts which, he said showed a profit of £785,000 before transfer fees were counted. Transfer fees turned this into a loss of £1.3 million. This was even with £600,000 from the Development Fund, effectively money from Celtic Pools. The club, he added, had the full support of the Bank but he did not mention the concern the Bank of Scotland had already expressed that the club's share capital was out of line with its debt. Instead he said that the club's professional advisers had examined proposals regarding the share capital and the directors had decided it would be increased. Another meeting would be held to do just this. That meeting, though, never took place.

Low was at the AGM to meet other shareholders and to gather information, if necessary by using the Companies Act to request minutes of meetings and copies of shareholders' lists. He was not there to rock the boat. But another man there was not afraid to tear into the board. Bill Gallacher was already angry with them and was one of the few shareholders who, even before the emergence of a rebel faction, had no qualms about standing up and lambasting the directors about matters trivial or important. Gallacher was the grandson of Patsy Gallacher. In a club whose history is crowded with memorable players, Patsy had been a legend among legends. Low took his phone number.

At the end of the meeting chief executive Terry Cassidy reviewed his plans for the future, ranging from official hamburger stands to a new stadium. Later shareholders tucked into chicken sati and drumsticks, washed down with white wine. Michael Kelly greeted Low and his friends with a cheery, if condescending, 'Hello, boys, what are you guys doing here?' He had no idea the proxies could speak for around 30 per cent of the company of which he was a director.

Early next evening Low and Doherty met Shennan at the Grosvenor Hotel on Glasgow's Great Western Road. Shennan was impatient to run a story but the two insisted that the conversation remained off the record. Later Low and Doherty went with Tom Grant and his wife to Charlie Nicholas's Cafe Cini. Grant was then all for pushing White and Kelly off the board and he was getting along famously with Doherty on his last night before returning to Canada. One director was on side for the time being. Could Jimmy Farrell now be brought over?

Four days before Christmas Low and Bill Gallacher met at Glasgow's Pond Hotel. Gallacher was in his late thirties. A joiner by trade and a heavy smoker by habit, he now ran a recruitment agency for HGV lorry drivers in Cumbernauld. Articulate and concerned about Celtic, he was one of those plain, straightforward men the West of Scotland produces in quantity and whom it is too easy to under estimate.

Gallacher's grandfather, Patsy, first appeared for Celtic in 1911 and immediately won admirers for both his dexterity with the ball and his guts in playing on immediately after a fierce tackle. In his first season he was in the team that won the Scottish Cup, scoring one of two goals in the final. Fourteen years later in the closing minutes of another final he averted defeat with a unique goal. Only five feet six inches he stumbled after a tough tackle just feet from Dundee's goal. But he kept hold of the ball with his feet and somersaulted the ball – and himself – into the net.

His grandson showed the same kind of courage in not backing away from a tackle. The usual reaction from shareholders to Low and Dempsey's plan was: 'It can't be done. White and Kelly have it sewn up.' It was the classic way that rulers stayed in power, keeping any potential opposition despairing and despondent. The first step had to be to bring them together, to give them hope, to show them that something could be done, that as shareholders they had rights. Gallacher already realised this and would not give up. But he did not have the knowledge or the expertise to take matters further and he was delighted to meet a fellow believer who had.

When he heard what Low and Dempsey had been doing, he was not only on their side but he was immediately one of the hawks. The plain man who lived in a high-rise flat in Cardonald, Glasgow, and the financial analyst who lived in an elegant West End townhouse hit it off and became friends as well as allies.

Bill Gallacher held 85 shares. He gave Low the phone number of his Uncle Tommy, also a shareholder, a son of the great Patsy and a former footballer himself, who now lived in Dundee. He too disliked the board for the way he had been treated in the past. The board had taken away privileges from the minority shareholders, privileges which cost the club almost nothing but were important to the shareholders. All they had received was a free stand seat and a guaranteed ticket for all away matches which they paid for. In a petty-minded action the board took these rights away because it was allegedly costing too much, even though few actually took up their rights. Many companies offer quite lucrative privileges to their shareholders, but Celtic could not afford the odd stand ticket, even when there were empty seats at Parkhead.

Low went to Dundee on Christmas Eve. The first thing that greeted him at Tommy Gallacher's house was a huge Alsatian that almost knocked him over. The second was a quiet, gentle man, very different from his nephew. Tommy had played for Clydebank and when he gave up the game became a journalist with the *Sunday Post* and the *Dundee Courier*. Another way Tommy differed from Bill was that he was sceptical: nothing could be done about the board. But over tea and biscuits he and his wife discussed Celtic with their visitor and he was pleased to offer his support. The two Gallachers pledged their 170 shares, adding another one per cent of the club to the cause.

Before returning to Glasgow Low called in on Angus Cook, then still the controversial Chairman of Dundee, in his office above the Parliamentary Bar which he also owned. Cook knew a great deal about a number of football clubs and liked to keep his ear to the ground. He had already heard something was building up at Celtic.

He was not the only one. Kevin McKenna, who was writing a piece for the *Irish News*, met Low the day before New Year's Eve but Low resolutely refused to confirm anything even though he was now meeting Dempsey three times a week.

The New Year began with a new target. Maureen Blackburn lived in Sussex and held 802 shares. She had not been approached before because the rebels knew nothing about her. If they did approach her and told her their plans, it could let the cat out of the bag and alert the board. Every approach until now had been to shareholders suspected of being sympathetic to the rebels' cause: if they were sympathetic, they were brought on side; if they were uninterested, an offer was made for their shares.

Maureen Blackburn was an unknown, but the time had come to make an attempt. She was a former pupil of Notre

Dame in Glasgow, though now in her mid-fifties, married to a former ICI executive, John Blackburn. What finally persuaded Low to make contact was the fact that she had transfered 100 shares to her husband, to her son Simon who lived in Hong Kong and her daughter Amanda. That might mean she was prepared to sell her shares or to gift them to avoid possible capital gains tax.

The first phone call brought good news. Michael Kelly had already expressed an interest in the shares and Low now had a chance to pick up four per cent of the club while denying it to the board. Mrs Blackburn was prepared to sell 400 of her shares, but she was asking £300 a share, an all-time record and 100 times the value that the board had put on shares only months earlier.

'That's an awfully high price, Maureen,' said Low. 'But we will buy the 400 at £300 a share on condition that you grant the proxy votes for all 800 shares.'

Mrs Blackburn agreed. The rebels were up to 36 per cent. but on another front, the news was less good. Fanzine editor Matt Mcglone told Low the gossip was almost out of control. *Daily Record* journalists had started going to Heraghty's Bar on the South Side trying to pick up information. That evening Shennan and Kevin McCarra met Low at his home. They told him bluntly they were going to run a story that Sunday with what they already knew on the record. They were giving him the chance to fill in the details.

Twelve hours later Low was with Dempsey for their morning meeting. 'There's a story coming out, Brian, and once it's out the shit's going to hit the fan. We must conclude that Maureen Blackburn deal before the story comes out.'

Low arranged to meet Mrs Blackburn at Gatwick Airport on Saturday 18 January. He boarded the 9 a.m. flight from Glasgow believing he had 24 hours before the story broke. He did not realise it was *Scotland on Sunday's* practice to put out a Press release the day before to radio and the other media.

The story would be incredible to many. Celtic had always been regarded as immune to any kind of takeover. Legend among the fans had it that it was protected by a little old lady in Ireland who was the main shareholder and she would never sell her shares. The lady who came closest to that description had been Felicia Grant, whose shares on her death had passed to relatives in Canada and Ireland. What had really protected the club, however, had been the board's veto on registering the transfer of shares which was now being ruthlessly exercised.

Nor was this a conventional business story. It was to be in effect a takeover without a bid. The plan was for an injection of £16.4 million into the club but this was not the same as a £16.4 million takeover. On the Saturday Shennan and McCarra liaised directly with *Scotland on Sunday* editor Andrew Jaspan to ensure the details were scrupulously correct. It could be portrayed by rivals as a story about an unknown with loud ties and braces and a vague-sounding financial job teaming up with a sacked director to take over a national institution which everyone knew could never be taken over; if they got it wrong they would never be allowed to forget it.

Under the headline 'Secret bid to stir up Celtic' and an exclusive tag, they reported the plan to dilute the control of the White and Kelly families and re-structure and re-finance the club, bringing it up to £16 million of new investment. Low insisted on being quoted as saying no more than: 'I don't want to get into confirming or denying any story you put to me.' Far from being, as some of the directors believed at the time, a carefully timed leak, the story was outside Dempsey and Low's control.

The stories which appeared on Page One and Page Six were checked and double-checked. Unfortunately a discrepancy crept into the much shorter Press release put out that Saturday. It would later lead to a very different story in another paper.

Meanwhile Low and the Blackburns were getting along famously. John and Maureen, a large, gregarious woman, had taken Low to their house in East Grinstead for lunch. She loved talking about Celtic, Glasgow and Notre Dame. She was annoyed with Michael Kelly who had lobbied her to support his joining the board 18 months before and had been in touch only periodically since. She had heard the accusations about Dempsey and Robroyston and Low gave her the other side of the story.

Over lunch with the couple and their daughter and son-in-law, accompanied by a generous serving of wine, they discussed what was wrong with the board. In fact they talked about Celtic all afternoon. They eventually concluded the deal for the shares and Low caught the train to London with the daughter and son-in-law. They offered him a room in their flat for the night, but he was still hoping to catch the last plane back to Glasgow. Tired from a long day and liberal glasses of wine at lunch, he eventually arrived at Glasgow airport.

A sudden flash of white light blinded him for a moment. Then a second, and a third. From one side of the two photographers came shouted questions with the words Celtic and takeover repeated. Shit! The story was wide open, the board would be alerted and they still had only 36 per cent of the votes at best. A copy of the *Scotland on Sunday* Press release was thrust at him. It was a long way from the full story. 'That's nonsense,' he said. The denial made the back page of the *Sunday Mail*.

Michael Kelly Associates responded with a Press release throwing cold water on the story. At its foot in a 'Note to editors' it pointed out that one of the story's authors. Shennan, a 'respected financial journalist', was known to be a business associate of David Low. This was no secret as Shennan had insisted on it being inserted in *CA* magazine when their analysis of Scottish football finance appeared.

In spite of both Dempsey and Low's fears, the story did not harm their cause. New supporters started appearing. It was as if an obstacle had been removed. Here were people who believed something could be done. The board did not have absolute power. There was hope of change. One of the new supporters for the takeover plan brought with him the aura of the best Celtic traditions. Lisbon Lion Jim Craig, who had shared a Save Our Celts platform with Dempsey, was also Jimmy Farrell's son-in-law. Now a dentist, one of a still-rare group of university-educated footballers, he was also an eloquent and knowledgeable commentator for the BBC. His status as a former player and Lisbon Lion was ideal for making contact with more shareholders.

Michael Kelly complained to the BBC that Craig could no longer be regarded as an independent commentator. Within a week, Craig's contract had been terminated. The effect, however, was simply to clear the way for him to be even more outspoken in the rebel cause.

Low approached another representative of Celtic tradition. Mrs Anne McLaughlin was related to one of the first families to subscribe for shares in Celtic Football and Athletic Company Ltd in 1987. She and her brother, Brian Fitzpatrick, had 121 shares each. Mrs McLaughlin, a primary school teacher at St Aloysius, met Low at her home in Newlands, Glasgow. She listened to what he had to say without expressing support or opposition. He knew nothing of her sympathies, but as the net was cast wider it was necessary to take more risks, to approach shareholders they knew little about.

It turned out that this particular shareholder had a long and close association with the Whites and the Kellys and her allegiances were very much with them. Her solicitors, Gordon & Smythe in Glasgow's Sauchiehall Street, had a long-standing association with White and with Celtic. She knew the club had problems but her loyalty to the White and Kelly families made her reluctant to support proposals for change.

Even professional advisors now wanted to speak to the rebels. Low and Dempsey were invited to the offices of accountants Pannell Kerr Forster, where Paul McNeill was a manager, for lunch with managing partner Raymond Blin. The firm had been Celtic's auditors until 1982 but had been replaced by Arbuckle & Co who were very friendly with the White family. In an unusual move, the new auditors later merged with the accountancy firm belonging to White, Celtic's largest shareholder, to become Desmond White, Arbuckle & Co. As auditors have to be independent, they were replaced by Hardie Caldwell.

Pannell Kerr Forster were also Fergus McCann's advisors. His earlier advisors, Touche Ross, also worked for Miller Construction who were putting forward a stadium reconstruction plan for Celtic. There was a potential conflict of interest, so Low introduced McCann to PKF.

From the start the object had been to put together a coalition, to reach agreement on the route to be taken and then to put it into action. Dempsey and John Keane had been there from the start and McCann had been pursuing a parallel course. Now a friend introduced Low to his former banker at the Royal Bank of Scotland, Dominic Keane, no relation to John. Dominic's brother , based in Bermuda, then wanted to become involved. The next step was to get the Dempsey-Keanes team to work with the McCann team.

By now the fans, shareholders and the media were talking openly about a takeover, but Dempsey and Low had not yet put the second stage of the plan into action. Until now the campaign had consisted only of collecting the support of shareholders. Now it was beginning to reach the point where they would ask for a meeting with the board to demand two seats. That would, of course, be refused but they had to go through the motions of asking. When the request was denied they would call an extraordinary general meeting to vote two people on to the board. Jim Doherty was planning to fly over from Canada on 13 February. That was the time to demand a meeting. The plan was working like clockwork except, that is, for the media.

Shennan had been in touch to see if any news story was likely to break that weekend. Low told him Scottish Television's chief football correspondent Gerry McNee wanted an interview with Doherty for Friday night's *Scotsport* programme 'but he won't be saying anything new'. Shennan had too much respect for McNee's interviewing skills and said Doherty could well say more than he intended.

Doherty flew into Glasgow on the afternoon of Thursday. One newspaper had described him, wrongly, as a millionaire but once that got into the cuttings libraries and became fixed in people's minds, his status was elevated to that of yachting tycoon instead of simply buying and selling yachts as a business, though the man himself did not contribute to the mistake. McNee sent a car to the airport to take him and Low, acting as his minder, to the Cowcaddens studios.

The interview went according to Low's plan at first. Doherty's comments were gentle, almost bland. The interview was almost over.

They paused. Then McNee started to put questions which were more leading, very gently coaxing good television out of Doherty. The Canadian admitted openly to planning to get White and Kelly off the board. There was an almost imperceptible buzz among the studio crew who knew they had something big. Everybody thought it was a 'cracking' interview, but Low thought it was bad news. McNee left the studio knowing he had a hot story. In fact, he had something more.

Doherty and Low went on to the Pond Hotel where they were to meet Bill Gallacher and Matt McGlone. After McGlone had interviewed the Canadian for *Once A Tim*, the three others crossed over to Carriages restaurant for a meal, where they were joined later by McCarra and Shennan. The restaurant manager came to the table to say 'the Press' were outside. A tabloid journalist had tried to come into the restaurant but the manager had locked the doors and told him it was closed. He invited Doherty and his companions to finish the meal in their own good time. Doherty was a celebrity that weekend and was being treated as such.

Next day Doherty and Low took the 12.50 p.m. flight to Belfast Harbour airport. In Low's case was a copy of the already drafted requisition for an EGM. It contained three resolutions: to put Brian Dempsey, David Low and Jim Doherty on to the board of Celtic Football Club.

Chapter Six

THE REBEL STRONGHOLD

In my eyes the most important aspect of winning is to reward Celtic supporters. I have come to understand why our supporters are so exceptional and so attached to this club . . . I am under no illusions of what is required.

— Liam Brady

I

IF there was a safe haven for Celtic rebels it was Cushendall on the Antrim coast. It played host to all the rebel leaders at various times and was the home of a number of shareholders. The Glens of Antrim Celtic Supporters Club elected Jim Doherty as their President and made Low a committee member. Kevin McCarra, a football writer with a classical education, christened it the home of the rebels' Praetorian Guard.

The town had a tendency to sympathise with rebels, being a nationalist area, although it was basically a gentle seaside town strung out around a simple main street. In summer the population doubled as visitors poured in from Belfast, 20 miles away. For Doherty, Low, Dempsey, McCann and the other visitors during the campaign for Celtic Football Club, there were two strategically important buildings in the town.

First was the Riverside Guest House where Pat and Anne McKeegan offered a welcoming, homely base and the kind of king-sized breakfast fry-up complete with potato scones necessary to aid recovery from the rigours of visiting the second building. This was The Central bar, owned by Oliver McMullen, husband of Sinead Neeson, Tom Grant's cousin. It was usually busy and the wood of the counter was worn smooth by the arms and elbows of decades of customers, drawn there by the atmosphere and a justifiably famous gantry. McMullen himself was an independent councillor, which is almost synonymous with nationalism in that area.

Before Doherty and Low could get there, however, they had work to do. The EGM was intended as a last resort but they knew well their request for seats on the board would be refused by Kevin Kelly and the other directors. The media were already discussing an EGM openly so the board were expecting it. The trip to the north of Ireland was to have the requisition signed by the necessary ten per cent of shareholders.

They were met at the airport by Aiden Neeson, McMullen's brother-in-law, in his black BMW and drove to Toomebridge and Portglenone to have the requisition and proxy forms signed. There was no hesitation by the shareholders, but it took up the rest of that St Valentine's Day. Then they set off for Cushendall. Soon they were in the warm fug and gentle crush of The Central bar.

It was after 10.30 p.m. when *Scotsport Extra Time* came on the television. Because the town is on the coast it picks up Scottish Television clearly. Doherty was at the bar ordering Budweisers when his face came up on the screen. A customer at the bar looked from the screen to the man next to him and back to the screen again. 'Fuck me, it's him,' he said. 'Hey, turn the television up. It's the big fella.'

Low's four-letter reaction to the screened interview was the same as the man discovering Doherty next to him in the bar. Here was Big Jim telling the world, and through the television the subjects themselves, that the rebels wanted Christopher White and Michael Kelly off the board. They had been too sure of themselves to act on the warning implicit in the media stories. Now it was being spelled out for them.

The interview was a significant event. Until now the rebels had engaged in guerilla warfare, gathering support and buying shares. That had now changed. McNee had a good interview and a hot story, all right, but to the board and the rebels it was also a declaration of war.

II

BACK in Scotland the directors also saw the programme. Michael Kelly at least would know the significance of it. He had seen what happened at Bremner, seen an in-fighter like Rowland-Jones defeated, seen Carswell's stockbroking firm shut down. This was serious. It was more than a media story. It was war and he knew what he was up against. By Sunday tea-time Tom Grant was round at Low's house. 'Did you see that programme?' he said.

That Sunday evening Grant and Low went to visit Mrs McLaughlin at her home in Newlands, accompanied by Doherty and Paul McNeill, who had been at St Aloysius' school with her son. Whether Grant realised it or not, this trip firmly marked him out as a threat to White and Kelly. It was one thing speaking out, but something else to be participating in an attempt to buy up shares for the opposition. McNeill had already spoken to her brother in Bath, Paul Fitzpatrick, and was negotiating to buy shares. Low had been pressing McNeill to conclude a deal. It was becoming a paper chase, to the cry of 'Get those shares'. The price agreed was £160 a share and Fitzpatrick was willing to sell to the rebels.

Mrs McLaughlin gave no indication she would not support them. She shared a lot of their views of the board and had been disappointed in Michael Kelly, having been lobbied for support when he went on to the board but had little contact since. But she was also disappointed to learn her brother was willing to sell. She wanted to buy some of his shares but could only afford 20 of them. She instructed her solicitors, Gordon & Smythe, to buy. Then Fitzpatrick told McNeill he had decided to keep his shares. Later, however, 81 partly-paid Paul Fitzpatrick shares were transferred to Michael Kelly and 40 fully-paid shares to his wife, Zita. Phone calls to Bath and Mrs McLaughlin confirmed they had been sold.

Another key stake of 268 shares belonged to Mrs Margaret Janetta, of Barrhead, an acquaintance of Jimmy Farrell, who the rebels believed had spoken to her about the shares. Instead she sold them, to Chris White.

Acquiring these shares would have taken the rebel holding over the crucial 50 per cent barrier. It was a week before the official appearance of David Smith. Both parcels of shares were shortly afterwards sold to the new deputy Chairman, allowing him to qualify as a director of Celtic. The loss of those shares – the first defeat for the rebels – and Smith's arrival were both prompted by that one television programme.

David Dallas Smith was born in Brechin and trained as an accountant in Glasgow with one of the firms which later became Ernst & Young, one of the smaller number of mega-firms in accountancy. He worked on the liquidation of Upper Clyde Shipbuilders before heading to more glamorous work in London, such as the Beatles' company Apple Corps at the time the group was splitting up. He worked on the unsuccessful side defending Perth-based Arthur Bell, maker of Bell's whisky, when Guinness launched its takeover bid in 1985, and later on the attacking side when supermarket chain William Low tried and failed to buy Safeway. He had a reputation for enjoying negotiating and complex deals. One tax advisor who knew him in his early days said: 'If there is a way out of a difficult situation which is dramatic, David will find it.'

It was after advising several supermarket groups that he put together a deal that made the financial world sit up and take notice. In April 1989 he launched a takeover bid for the Gateway chain that would eventually cost £2,130 million, the biggest in British corporate history. By far the largest part of the money was borrowed in one form or another. The technical term for it was a 'leveraged buy-out'. The principle was simple but it was difficult to pull off. What you did was borrow the money against the value of the company you were buying. You sold off bits of the target company to bring your debt down. Then you would use the profits from the remaining part of your company to pay the interest or, eventually, sell shares in it on the stock market and use that money to pay off the borrowings.

But the scale of what Smith did raised a lot of eyebrows and made his company's name, Isosceles, a regular in *Financial Times* headlines. He was in effect bringing an American technique into Britain which had already earned a bad name in the States. If you borrowed too much money for the takeover, you might be left short of money to repay the loans or pay the interest on them afterwards. Isosceles came as close to coming unstuck as anyone can comfortably get without going over the edge. It was more difficult than expected to sell bits of the company to bring the debt down. Smith had managed to borrow the money at fixed interest rates, but even with the rates pegged the profits from the Gateway supermarkets were only just enough to pay the interest on the loans.

Smith and his business partner Liz Hignall later agreed to leave the company with a pay off of £1.8 million between them. Three years after the deal Isosceles was still struggling with debts of £1,300 million and was in danger of breaking the conditions of its loans from the bank. Three months after Smith joined Celtic it emerged that Isosceles was also unable to pay interest in cash on £290 million of the debt and instead was offering shares or cash at a future date.

The new chief executive of Isosceles told the *Financial Times* that Smith and Hignall put together projections which showed the company could generate a healthy return on its investment but they based their calculations on American experience and failed to understand the British market.

White and Kelly knew they needed a white knight. White had been trained at another of the accountancy firms which became part of Ernst & Young, as did one of his closest friends and a Celtic shareholder, Francis McCrossan, who knew Smith. The board had discussed Smith, and other candidates, before. Jack McGinn had known him for ten years but when it came to the board meeting to co-opt Smith on 21 February he voted against his co-option. So did Jimmy Farrell and Tom Grant. Michael Kelly was particularly keen to bring him on. After the Doherty interview with McNee, he felt he was picked out as a target by the rebels. Kelly, his cousin Kevin and White were the only directors who voted for Smith. It was Kevin Kelly, using his casting vote as Chairman, who brought him on to the board. Normal business practice was for a Chairman to use his casting vote to maintain the status quo or to leave the board's options as open as possible until they could vote by a simple majority. A Chairman could use his casting vote to initiate change if he felt there was no time for the matter to be looked at again, but this was usually in exceptional circumstances.

It was the first defensive move the board had made. Smith's presence was a sign that the directors realised they could not solve their problems themselves. He was voted on as an ordinary director but, in spite of the fact that the vote split the board right down the middle, he was almost immediately made deputy Chairman of the company. So not only was his appointment unusual but so was his promotion.

III

THE next stage of the campaign required a meeting with the Chairman. Spokesmen for a large minority shareholding who did not feel they were fairly represented on the board would normally approach the Chairman to ask for representation in the form of seats on the board. On 14 February 1992 Low sent Kevin Kelly an unusual Valentine. It was a fax he had prepared for Doherty expressing serious concern about the club and arranging a meeting at Parkhead. 'I am returning to Canada on Wednesday,' it read, 'and it is of crucial importance to you and the club that we are able to have a meeting.'

Before the meeting, though, they approached someone they knew the Chairman listened to. That man was Jim Torbett, owner of The Trophy Centre group of shops which employed Kevin Kelly. Doherty and Low met him at the Tinto Firs Hotel on Glasgow's South Side on 17 February. Again they outlined their case. Torbett remained non-committal.

Their meeting with Kelly was arranged for 10 a.m. on 18 February, but the Press were already on to the story. The night before Doherty, Low, Brian Dempsey and Tom Grant were to have a meal together in the Amber Regent restaurant in West Regent Street. Grant brought news from Kelly that the meeting had been switched from Parkhead to the Westerwood hotel in Cumbernauld to try and throw off the reporters.

The attempt resulted in a farce worthy of Peter Sellars, with Kelly circling a roundabout twice in his car pursued by reporters, going back to his house, leaving again, stopping to buy a newspaper. Eventually he reached Westerwood, a modern version of an upmarket hotel. He met Doherty first before Kelly asked if Low, who was sitting some distance off, would like to join them.

Kelly was anxious to talk about anything but the issue. He complained about the Press interest. He talked about his own health, about his Uncle Bob, about how the Lisbon Lions were more Sir Robert Kelly's creation than Jock Stein's. Low gave him the message he had given the shareholders. 'This is a crucial time in the club's history, Kevin. At this crucial time it is important that the interests of as many shareholders as possible are represented.' Things were going wrong with the club and things were going to get worse. Low did not say they wanted to remove anybody, but they did ask for two seats on the board, without mentioning any names, otherwise there was 'a good prospect' of an EGM. Kelly was shown some of the proxies they already had for requisitioning the meeting, so he would know they were serious. As an added precaution, Low secretly tape-recorded the meeting, which produced little but bad publicity afterwards.

The meeting was followed up with a letter to Kelly from Doherty summing up the rebels' requests:

As you saw we hold irrevocable proxies in favour of over 30 per cent of the club's shares. At this pivotal time in the club's history it is only proper that the views of all shareholders are fully represented. We are requesting two additional seats on the board. You undertook to ensure that our proposals would be discussed to conclusion at your next board meeting.

The undertaking mentioned in the last sentence meant the board could not stall. They had to make a decision for or against at their next meeting.

Kelly told the board that Doherty had said that Michael

Kelly must be removed immediately, possibly along with Chris White and another unnamed director, and Doherty, Low and later Dempsey were to come on the board. This was not said when the three of them were together at the Westerwood. The request was only for two seats on the board, no candidates were mentioned and no names were put forward for removal. Kelly reported that they were prepared to call an EGM, but rather than disrupt the club they would call it at the end of the season.

The board split down the middle on whether or not to meet Doherty and Low, with Grant, Farrell and McGinn being in favour. Kelly used his casting vote to squash the idea. When they voted on whether to co-opt Doherty and Low on to the board, there was again the same split and again the same casting vote. Minutes later the board voted on the co-option of David Smith. Yet again there was the same split on the board, but this time the casting vote went in favour of bringing Smith on. Events might have taken a very different course if Kelly had shown more courage and initiative.

Low wrote to congratulate Smith on his appointment, although adding that the circumstances were of concern, and suggested a meeting to exchange views. Instead Smith asked for any 'positive suggestions' to be put in writing.

The next Saturday Celtic met Hibs at Easter Road. Chris White was openly and loudly abused by fans who called him a 'swine', 'ratbag', and even stronger epithets. 'Why the hell don't you resign?' shouted one. Only feet away Dempsey was engulfed in good wishes and proffered hands to shake.

Low went along as the guest of Kevin Doyle, an Edinburgh businessman who had recently made a handsome profit on shares in a company called Waverley Cameron in a battle of nerves with former Argyll stores boss Jimmy Gulliver. It was Low who originally sold him the shares. Though a Celtic fan, Doyle's companies had executive facilities at both Easter Road and Tynecastle. Low found himself in the box right next to that of the Celtic directors. When he saw Cassidy coming in, he shouted mischievously: 'How's it going, Terry?'

After the game – which Celtic won 0-2 – Cassidy and Low again found themselves face-to-face as part of a phone-in for

Radio Clyde. Cassidy became more ruffled and outspoken as it went on. He claimed Low, Doherty and Dempsey lacked 'talent, money, anything'. At one point he said of them: 'Why don't these people go away and play with the traffic?' It was such a lively piece of radio it later won a silver medal in the live phone-in section of the Sony Awards, the equivalent of the British radio Oscars. It was beaten for the gold award only by a BBC national radio programme. In a mood of devilment Low asked Cassidy for his autograph as soon as the programme ended. Everybody started laughing but Cassidy walked off in a huff.

The following week White and Kelly decided not to wait for the rebels' EGM to strike first. They requisitioned an EGM themselves, Celtic's first since 1948. The object, was to remove Tom Grant and Jimmy Farrell.

In the run-up to the EGM, Fergus McCann flew over from Montreal and checked into the Central Hotel, a comfortable once grand hotel above the city's main station. The Press were covering the story extensively but it was again Gerry McNee who tracked down McCann. Instead of just 'doorstepping' the hotel – waiting outside with camera ready – he doorstepped McCann's hotel room. The dapper Canadian stepped out of his door to be confronted by a television lens and the news that McNee was going to broadcast a report whether he was given an interview or not. They went downstairs to the lounge for an interview but McCann was more shrewd than Doherty and gave nothing away.

McCann still believed the best route to wresting control of Celtic from the ruling families was to set up a new, parallel company. Celtic's Future plc would be a public company in which the fans would buy shares, raising £5 million. He himself would inject a huge cash sum and take a majority control. The existence of this company, if it had the overwhelming support of the fans, on top of the club's financial problems would put enormous pressure on the board to agree to be taken over by Celtic's Future plc.

The plan was picked over by the professional advisors of both teams in meetings at PKF and stockbrokers Greig Middleton. Low introduced McCann to the Henry Ansbacher merchant bank which had produced the prospectus for the Manchester United flotation. While McCann was becoming keener and pushing hard for his chosen route, Low was becoming more sceptical. The two teams were drifting further apart, not closer. And there was still an EGM to fight.

Chapter Seven

THE EMPIRE
STRIKES BACK

Winning trophies is a necessity for this club. It is necessary
to maintain the club's high profile and reputation worldwide.
It is necessary too for financial reasons: a winning team
attracts bigger crowds, better sponsorships and lucrative
television deals.

– Liam Brady

I

THE Extraordinary General Meeting was to be the first set-
piece battle of the campaign. Shareholders would be asked
to vote on the attempt by the White-Kelly dynasty to dump
two directors whose offence seemed to be putting allegiance
to the club over allegiance to the dynasty. They would argue
that directors who opposed them or revealed information
about the company could not remain on the board. But
subject to clear legal limits, it was sometimes the duty of a
director to oppose his fellow directors. This was to be a
crucial test of strength for both sides. Could this tightly knit
group within the board rule unfettered or could other
shareholders, acting together, draw a line around what they
could do?

Almost unnoticed in the week that the date of the EGM
was set by the board, Brian Dempsey lodged plans for a

multi-million pound housing project at Robroyston. Re-zoning consent had already been granted by the Regional Council, making the land available for housing. The same little group that was masterminding the EGM had cut Celtic out of the chance to participate in the development of Robroyston.

Immediately after the board meeting at which Kelly and White revealed they were calling an EGM, Tom Grant, Jack McGinn and Jimmy Farrell were down at Brian Dempsey's office at different times. The building was like a general headquarters on the eve of battle with journalists and shareholders coming and going. Tom Grant even recorded a television interview with Chick Young in Dempsey's office .

When the to-ing and fro-ing subsided, Dempsey, Low, Grant and Farrell formed a war cabinet to plan their tactics in the month before the EGM. The first thing was to examine their own share base. They had 40 per cent of the votes; they needed 50 per cent to defeat the three resolutions which would be put to the meeting: to co-opt Smith, and to remove Grant and Farrell. The share-buying must continue. Low was to organise all the proxies to oppose the resolutions. That meant returning to Cushendall, but as well as beers at The Central, and breakfast at the Riverside Guest House he also managed to acquire a few more shares. Every share counted now.

Unfortunately Farrell had already given away a penalty. His daughter Liz, and son-in-law, Jim Craig had been given shares and wanted them transferred. Chris White had agreed to put the transfer through, but Farrell had overlooked a small but critical point: shares had to be registered for 30 days before the new holder of the shares could vote. White's apparently reasonable agreement to transferring the shares disqualified the votes that went with them from being used at the EGM.

The team of advisors was beefed up with Dominic, John and Eddy Keane becoming more closely involved, and Brendan Somers, former manager of the Allied Irish Bank in Glasgow, and veteran solicitor Len Murray were added. As the EGM approached, tensions rose. Low became more aggressive and increasingly inpatient with Farrell. They had to play to win. There was no room for prevarication. They had to buy more shares and disrupt the opposition. It would be an uphill stuggle and very difficult to win, but not impossible. As the Americans say: 'The opera ain't over 'til the fat lady sings.'

Grant felt the pressure most. As an employee of the club as well as a director, doing a job he loved, a young man who had just taken out a mortgage on a new house where he hoped to make a home for two adopted boys, he had the most to lose. He was a good man at heart who believed it should have been possible to patch up their differences with the men trying to dump him from the board. He was looking for a way to act as a peacemaker. He also knew that the maximum strength of the rebels was not enough.

Somers was sent to the north of Ireland in pursuit of more shares. Farrell prompted Dempsey and John Keane to throw money at the problem, to offer ever increasing prices for opposition shares. They made an unsuccessful offer to Adele Daly, Chris White's aunt and sister of the former Chairman, of £500 a share although the general price was £300.

The dynasty had scored an own goal with the timing of the meeting. It would fall on the eve of the Tennents Scottish Cup semi-final against Rangers. It was difficult to imagine a more important match in any season but for a club whose fans were suffering from trophy starvation this was critical. It brought back memories of the AGM that ousted Brian Dempsey which fell two days before a Skol Cup final – which Celtic lost.

It also brought together the disparate pressure groups into a united front, under the name Celts for Change. Although it involved fanzine editor Matt McGlone, it was not the same organisation that emerged under that name in the following year. It was a looser coalition of Save Our Celts, the Independent Celtic Supporters Association and subscribers to the fanzines *Once A Tim* and *Not The View*. It planned a 'wanted' poster campaign against White and the Kellys.

But their impact would be limited. Low wrote to Save Our Celts: 'With respect to S.O.C., the fanzines and other pressure groups, you are just that – pressure groups. Unless you agreed to a prolonged boycott you would not bring about change. Remember there are those within the board who would settle for 20 fallow years rather than relinquish control.'

With the best will in the world the fans at this stage could only try to influence the shareholders. It was among the shareholders that the battle had to be won. Ranged against the rebels were a formidable pile of shares. Chris White remained the largest shareholder with 2,952, Michael Kelly controlled 2,152 directly or indirectly and Kevin 1,787. Even with the other three directors siding with Dempsey, Doherty and Low, their best estimate of support was 47.5 per cent.

Tom Grant was given a crash course in company law. Low drafted a letter for him to sign and post to the club:

I propose to attend at the Registered Office on 13 March 1992 at 10.30 a.m., and if necessary on subsequent occasions, for the purpose of inspecting the accounting records of The Celtic Football and Athletic Company Ltd and you are requested to ensure that the following are accessible and available for inspection.

There followed a shopping list of demands made under the powers that the Companies Act gave to shareholders and directors. What the letter demanded was that all accounts required by law would be open for inspection along with all files on transactions with directors or their associates; that a shorthand writer and independent scrutineers would be arranged for the EGM; that the scrutineers would keep all papers from the meeting for at least 12 months; and that the club would arrange for a statement by Grant to be read out at the meeting.

The demand for accounts and files was really a trawl for any information that might supply ammunition for the battle. The demand about arrangements for the meeting was to provide a record to ensure that everything complied with the law or could be challenged later if it did not.

In the last week before the meeting they were still not in a position to win. Low was desperately looking for technical ways to stave off defeat, looking at how to stop people voting. He suggested that Farrell take him to the company secretary's office to look at the documents that had to be kept by law, such as share transfers. As a director, Farrell was legally entitled to see them. Low would go along as his assistant.

At the 8 a.m. war cabinet meeting in Dempsey's office on Friday, 27 March, only three days before the EGM, Low's lawyer Sandy Moffat was present. A director of Falkirk football club and 'a corporate ace', he had worked extensively on the Bremner battle. Farrell and Low were to go to the Celtic company secretary's office and if they found anything there Moffat was to expect a call before he returned to his Edinburgh office.

In the office of Desmond White Arbuckle & Co at 28 Bath Street, the two-man fishing expedition was greeted by Mr Arbuckle, a polite, over-weight gentleman, now balding and nearing retirement age. He was very helpful and they had no problem seeing the documents they were entitled to. The problem was a clash of philosophies between the two allies. Farrell was a lawyer and saw the rules as setting limits on what he could do. Low was a corporate advisor whose duty was to help those he was advising and the rules were part of his ammunition. He had told Farrell the documents he needed to see. Now having got them, Farrell would not let him see them all.

Among the documents Low had asked for were details of all share transfers in the last 30 years. They had to be dug out of the archive. While Farrell saw to that, Low looked at as many documents as he could, entitled to or not. He had been reminding his fellow rebels for weeks that they were playing to win. This was food and drink to him. He was practising what he preached.

Low reached Moffat on his mobile phone and they met in the unlikely setting of the Casey Jones burger bar in Queen Street station before the lawyer caught the Edinburgh train. Perched uncomfortably on plastic seats, drinking coffee from Polystyrene cups and eating a bun off cardboard plates, they leafed through copies of the statutory records of Celtic Football and Athletic Company Ltd.

'For fuck's sake, look at this, Sandy.' They had hit the jackpot with the share transfers. Ever since the 1963 Stock Transfer Act, partly-paid shares – those for which the full face-value had not yet been paid – had to be transferred on different forms from fully-paid shares. Celtic had simply carried on transferring partly-paid shares on the same forms as fully-paid shares. To the outsider it would seem to be a technicality, but the law is made up of a series of technicalities, and this breach had been going on for 30 years. Bingo!

Partly-paid shares had been unlawfully transferred and they could apply to the courts for an interim interdict – a provisional court order – to stop the holders of those shares voting. For the first time it looked as though they could defeat the resolutions at the EGM.

II

MOFFAT returned to Edinburgh to find an advocate to take their case to the Court of Session. Farrell suggested John Baird, an old St Aloysius boy and, not suprisingly, a Celtic fan. A meeting was arranged for that afternoon in Edinburgh. Baird was initially sceptical. Again there was a clash of philosophies. The advocate was advising cautiously, warning why an application for an interim interdict might fail. Low did not want to hear all the reasons why it might fail, he wanted to hear all the reasons why it could succeed. He wanted someone who could go into court as enthusiastic and gung-ho as he was. Moffat calmed him down a little. 'You can't tell Counsel to fuck off, David,' he whispered. He meticulously took Baird through their case and the advocate picked up some of their enthusiasm.

Back in Glasgow Low and Dempsey had other matters to deal with. McCann had decided to announce his plans for Celtic's Future plc. But they still had more pressing decisions to take. They had decided to apply for the interdict on the Sunday in Dempsey's name, as a registered shareholder in the club, and chose John Mitchell, QC, as senior counsel. If they were to argue that partly-paid shares should be disqualified, they would have to ask for a court order against substantial number of their own supporters as well as the board's.

The main worry now was caveats. A 'caveat' – like many legal terms it comes from the Latin, often badly translated – means a warning. Interim interdicts are designed to deal with urgent cases, where waiting for a full hearing would mean acting too late. The court is asked to take a decision there and then. There is no time to hear a fully prepared case from both sides: that can come later. But if you believe someone is likely to want an interdict against you, you can ask your lawyer to lodge a caveat with a court so that you will be warned in time.

The rebels found out who had caveats lodged. They would be left out of the case so they were not forewarned of the action. White had a caveat lodged, so although he was the largest shareholder with a large number of partly-paid shares, he was omitted from the case. The petition for the interdict listed other holders of partly-paid shares and the interdict would be served on them.

Celtic's constitution said proxies must be lodged 24 hours in advance and by 2 p.m. on the Sunday all rebel proxies were in. The board would be able to see the rebels had support from around 40 per cent of the shares. Around the same time the interim interdict was being granted. Before Sunday lunch-time was fully over, White and Kelly knew they had problems, big problems.

That night the dynasty held their own council of war. Dr Hugh Drake, an English-based shareholder in town for the EGM, bumped into a hurrying Tom Grant who ducked into a doorway hoping to avoid being spotted. The next person Drake spotted was Kevin Kelly.

Their war council consisted of the Kellys, White, Grant and representatives of various legal firms, Gordon Smythe, McGrigor Donald and Dickson Minto. The directors knew they had to act. That night the voting pact was spawned. It was officially called a Shareholders' Trust, though it was limited to only White, Grant and Michael and Kevin Kelly. It was soon dubbed 'the Trust of mistrust' as there was dislike and mutual suspicion among the four. Dr Drake would call it the Non-Aggression Pact after the infamous agreement between Hitler and Stalin. Legally it took the form of a limited company, called Celtic Nominees Ltd. So four of the six directors of Celtic – soon to be five out of seven – and the majority of the club's shares were bound together in another company.

Grant and his shares had now been neutralised but White and Kelly still wanted rid of Farrell. This was not the same as pushing aside a newly appointed director like Brian Dempsey. This was a man with three decades of service to the club: six years founding and running the Development Fund and another 27 years on the board itself. When Farrell joined the board, White and Kelly were still schoolboys. He would not walk away as quietly as Dempsey had done. Approaches were made to Farrell in the hope of keeping him quiet, three of them in the 24 hours before the EGM.

The last rebel war cabinet meeting before the EGM was at the usual time of 8 a.m. in Dempsey's office. The final preparations were made. Grant knew they should win that day but his fear was for the future. Even if they defeated White and Kelly this time, they could come back and try again. What happened then? Low, John and Eddy Keane agreed to underwrite Grant's salary for two years if necessary. But events were moving too fast to make him feel secure. Those who were not used to the pace were out of their depth. Grant left as quickly as possible and by the time he did they knew his support was doubtful.

During their meeting there was a call to say the other directors wanted to talk. Throughout the four weeks from the calling of the EGM, when they thought they held the winning ticket, they did not want to deal. Now they wanted a meeting that morning. At 11 a.m. – literally the 11th hour – Dempsey and Len Murray met them. The Kellys and White were prepared to make Farrell an honorary director, whatever that meant. He would be allowed a seat in the stand, a seat on the team bus for away games, tickets for cup finals and one for the European Cup final if Celtic ever reached one again. Farrell was furious. Celtic meant more to him than seats on a bus or in the stand. There would be no 11th hour deal. This fight would go the distance.

Chapter Eight

DALLAS AND DYNASTY

The rewards that go with being successful mean that the club can keep the bank manager satisfied, be active in a very competitive transfer market and be in a good position to pay the wages necessary to hold the players who are valuable assets to the club.

— Liam Brady

FOR David Dallas Smith to join with the dynasty controlling Celtic, his appointment had to be ratified by the shareholders. The closest most of these shareholders had ever come to a boardroom battle before were the television series *Dallas* and *Dynasty*. But on television, glossy fictional characters wheeled and dealed with ease, without a crease in their suits or a hair out of place. Now for the shareholders, and for millions of newspaper readers and television viewers, a boardroom battle was being fought out almost on their doorsteps, in a company they knew and cared about. Fans or not, few of them failed to have an opinion. And this time the lives of real people were at stake. The shareholders' decision that night would affect the whole future of Celtic.

There was some glitz at Parkhead that night. The rebels hired a Rolls Royce to arrive for the meeting. It was a touch of bravado. The outcome would have a serious psychological impact for both sides so a little morale-boosting was justified.

Kevin Sweeney, a partner with Celtic solicitors McGrigor Donald, had first to report to the EGM on the effect of the legal action. The club had received a copy of the Court of Session Petition only hours before the meeting. Sweeney said that 19 shareholders who were the subject of the court order would not be able to use the votes that went with their partly-paid shares. But in the interests of fairness the 13 shareholders who were not subject to the order but also held improperly registered shares would also have those votes disallowed.

The Chairman moved straight to Smith's ratification and invited him to speak. Only a few days earlier Jimmy Farrell had written to shareholders pointing out the heavy losses Smith's company Isosceles had made in its first two years and the pay-off made to him. Smith said Farrell was factually correct but his interpretation of events was wrong.

'What may be surprising to Jim is that in putting the thing together we had anticipated and indeed budgeted for the loss to be some £50 million worse than that,' he said. The performance of the main part of Isosceles, Gateway supermarkets, had improved by 50 per cent, the group had invested £150 million and had repaid more than £900 million of borrowings.

'This is the thing that is of real relevance as far as Celtic Football Club is concerned: it was done through rigorous financial control; it was done through prudence and foresight in the managing of the funding at a time when we an unprecedented period of high interest rates which brought the demise of many companies . . .

'Over the last 27 years Jim has been a director of this board, these are the very abilities which have been lacking in this football club. That is why we have seen a long period of piecemeal and short-term investment . . .'

The payments Smith had received from Isosceles, he was 'delighted to say', had been considerably higher than Farrell said. 'The contract of employment I had with Isosceles, unlike normal contracts of employment, had a right for me to leave at any time and to demand the entire contract to be paid in full.' That was because of the financial institutions bank-rolling the company 'insisted that I be there' and he left only because of a disagreement with the major shareholder. He ended with a dig 'in the nicest possible way' about Farrell being 'unlikely to have a career as a financial journalist'.

It was an arrogant debut. Lisbon Lion Jim Craig asked how Smith could consider working with people he accused of presiding over piecemeal investment. And was he so desperate to be on the board that he would not speak to the directors who opposed his appointment? Smith replied that he wanted to help the club 'achieve something better', and he had made himself available to Farrell but had not been taken up on the offer.

Farrell had repeatedly phoned Smith in London and at Parkhead the previous week but he was always in meetings. The one time Smith got back to him, Farrell was out. They finally bumped into each other at Ibrox the previous Saturday. 'I would have liked the opportunity to preserve good manners, to meet the man and discuss it before this thing was railroaded on to the other directors,' said Farrell. 'It was discussed among a cabal of three, possibly four, within the Celtic board with no forewarning.

'As for David Smith coming to meet the board which he did about 18 or 19 months ago, at that time his star was in the ascendant and he looked to be a reasonable candidate, although others were chosen – one very regrettably in my view . . . If I have said anything inaccurate in that letter, that is entirely his fault because he didn't explain himself to me.'

Low, as proxy for Jim Doherty, fired a series of questions at the board: 'How many shareholders have had the opportunity to find out what Mr Smith stands for? We don't know whether he is an executive director, a non-executive director, deputy Chairman or not. We don't know anything. Will he have a service contract? If so, how much money will he earn from the club? Will he be putting any money into the club? We cannot make a decision on this unless we have the facts. We have no facts at all. It is disgraceful and no way to run a company. Indeed, is he a shareholder?' Smith needed ten shares to qualify as a director.

'I have been appointed as a non-executive director,' said Smith. 'There are no financial arrangements of any kind between myself and the club, full stop.'

Low persisted. 'Will there be any financial arrangements between yourself and the club, and are you a shareholder?'

Chris White intervened. 'There are no plans for special arrangements with Mr Smith regarding a service contract or anything like that and his shareholding requirements will be fulfilled . . .

'Is he a shareholder just now?'

'No, he is not . . .'

'Mr Chairman, if Mr Smith is not a shareholder is the resolution to appoint him today competent?' Celtic's lawyer assured him it was: Smith had three weeks to acquire the shares he needed to be a director.

Smith's appointment was put to a show of hands, where it was defeated by 22 votes to 28. But because of the complications of disqualifying the holders of partly-paid shares, from voting, a poll vote had already been arranged.

Confused shareholders had to ask if they could vote or not. A shareholder who had inherited two shares from his grandfather 43 years earlier was told he could not vote. If you needed ten shares to vote, could you put your shares with someone else's to make ten? No.

Eventually everyone with ten or more shares was allowed to vote and the scrutineers went through the names and disqualified the votes that went with partly-paid shares. Celtic had never seen anything like it at an AGM.

While the poll vote was under way, Kevin Kelly made an announcement: 'The major shareholders of the club have reached an agreement whereby they have submerged their personal interests in order to bring a sense of stability to the board and to allow the board to operate free from concerns of ownership.' He was announcing the formation of the Shareholders' Trust, or voting pact, of five directors. With Tom Grant locked into that, they would vote against the resolution to remove him and recommended other shareholders to do the same. They needed little encouragement. On a show of hands it was defeated by 49 votes to nil. But the lawyer still insisted it went to a poll vote. 'I am sorry about it,' said Sweeney. 'You have got to thank the Pursuer in the Petition [that is, Dempsey] for yet another delay.'

Len Murray, himself a lawyer, speaking for Dempsey, objected: 'It is not due to the Petition at all. It is due to the total mess of the register of this company!'

The third resolution was to remove James Matthew Farrell. He asked Kevin Kelly as Chairman to read out a statement he had prepared. There was an irony in what followed coming from Kelly's lips:

Since you are about to vote on a resolution to remove me from the position of director, which I have held since 1964, the Companies Act allows me to make this statement.

I am not pleading for my job. It is true that I have been a Celtic supporter for 70 years. My family holds about four per cent of the Celtic shares, and I have worked for Celtic for 32 years. The real issue is whether the White/Kelly axis is to be allowed to control Celtic. You may say the White/Kelly axis has been in control for so long that it dosen't matter, but I think it does.

Firstly, Celtic has serious problems with over £4 million debt and the need to upgrade or build a new stadium. These issues are too important to leave to the axis. Secondly – and I regret to say this – the arrival of Michael Kelly as a director in May 1990 marked a change from the days when everyone worked together for Celtic to a more aggressive style more appropriate to people working with their own businesses.

Tom Grant and I are accused of dissent from the axis ideas and proposals. I say Tom Grant and I are doing our job in asking questions to try and get information on the ideas and proposals, because there is too much at stake.

I would suggest Celtic need independent directors who are not frightened to question and probe for information, to stand up for the small shareholders and supporters and to act as custodians for the future of Celtic. A competent, confident and open management welcomes this. A weak, nervous and secretive management does not.

I have worked as a solicitor in Glasgow for over 40 years. You learn a lot in that time. I think you, the small shareholder, need me or someone like me.

It was a dignified but powerful statement. At an emotional level it identified the Kellys and Whites as the 'axis', and by implication their opponents as the allies. It openly characterised White and Kelly as a bloc within the board working with their own methods . . . methods which were 'un-Celtic'. It squarely blamed Michael Kelly for introducing an aggressive style that conflicted with the traditional team approach.

Oddly the accusation against Kelly contrasted with how former employees remember him at Michael Kelly Associates. He appears to have given them their head and allowed them to get on with the job. None of them used the term 'aggressive' to describe his style there.

Farrell's timing, though, could not have been better. The Chairman had only just announced the creation of the voting pact by 'the major shareholders of the club' which would 'allow the board to operate free from concerns of ownership'. Minutes later here was Jimmy Farrell, veteran supporter, shareholder, ex-employee, director, and old-fashioned family lawyer, offering himself as the champion of the small shareholder: 'You need me or someone like me.'

When Kevin Kelly invited him to add to his statement, his tone and the accuracy of his broadside was unchanged. How pleased he was that Tom Grant was remaining on the board. 'I never knew why he was off, except that he had the courage to stand up to those directors who were trying to rule the club with a brusque authority and without proper consultation or information being given to the directors.'

The same directors who now wanted Grant out had, only months before, appealed on his behalf to Terry Cassidy because of his ability and hard work in looking after the stadium. He had just adopted two young boys, said Farrell, adding: 'His financial future hopefully will be settled for all time and there will be no repetition of what in my view was quite disgraceful conduct!'

Farrell then showed how little age had dimmed his wily intelligence. 'Now, why am I here left alone?' he asked, a director for 27 years, before which he ran Celtic Pools for nothing, a Celtic supporter and the only man on the board to have played on Celtic Park. He proceeded to answer his own question. 'All that I have done, as I have said in that statement, is resisted Michael Kelly, because he is the man who in my view should be ejected from this board! He has caused unbelievable disruption. He has been paid a handsome salary, admittedly under contract, for public relations, and in my view the public relations of this football club in the past 18 months or two years have never been lower!

'If I am voted off today, those directors who are with him, unless he changes his tune completely, will find him a most uneasy bedfellow, and they will not rest in their beds at night for imagining what he is up to.'

The old warhorse now turned deftly to the stadium consultants. In May 1991, six months after the door was slammed on Dempsey's offer of Robroyston, a firm of consultants called Superstadia Ltd had been appointed to carry out a detailed feasibility study of sites in the Greater Glasgow area. In January 1992 they reported back recommending Cambuslang as 'the preferred option'. The board had accepted Superstadia's recommendations and a move to Cambuslang, subject to Superstadia proving the project was financially viable.

'Superstadia worries the life out of me,' said Farrell. He, Jack McGinn and Brian Dempsey, while he was still a director, had met the leader of Superstadia only to be 'totally disappointed' with that he put forward. 'We have had no independent financial advice, unless something has happened in the last fortnight that I know nothing of . . . I am not at all happy with the contract we have entered into . . . certainly we have got no separate independent technical advice of any kind.'

Farrell had been involved with the re-roofing of the stand 20 years earlier. 'We made a mistake in 1971 in not getting independent technical advice . . . and we are repeating our mistake, we are doing exactly the same thing.'

He had raised the subject of Superstadia's contract with the board but, in spite of interest by Grant and McGinn, received no support. 'There were other alternatives . . . which were open to us, and many of us would like to remain at Celtic Park. If we don't do something, we are going into a minefield here – There are bound to be extras, and we could be looking at a total bill of £120 million . . .'

Farrell then revealed the existence of an alternative plan which he alleged had been hidden from him. His copy said it had been presented to him on 19 August 1991 but it had been put in a drawer. It was seven months later, at the beginning of March 1992, that he had finally been handed the copy.

'I have had it looked at by myself and other experts, and it is well worth considering. I am not arguing for this one particularly, I am not saying that there is something wrong with Superstadia, but I am saying it would appear to me that this has been concealed from the directors, and I think that is totally and utterly scandalous. I am saying that this is the way this club is being run . . .'

He revealed how the club's Bank and lawyers had warned of the need for increased capital. He had opposed a plan for injecting £500,000 as 'tinkering with the problem' and as detrimental to smaller shareholders who could not afford to buy the shares which would be on offer to them.

Farrell then exposed the attempts made to silence him. 'There have been three attempts for me to call off the dogs in the last 24 hours. Propositions have been put to me which are laughable and insulting. After 27 years and six years before that on the Development Fund, to retire with dignity, to get a ticket on the bus, to get tickets to Cup finals – to be allowed to go to one European Cup final! I will be there myself without any help!

'These things are a mockery of all Celtic stands for. Celtic always were a class act. Celtic were something different, where the directors and shareholders of Celtic Football Club were a fine body of men and women, and even on bad days when we weren't doing so well on the field everybody throughout the length and breadth of Scotland, and internationally, respected the Celtic for being a class apart.'

Grant was the first to back up Farrell. 'Jimmy has shown today why he should be retained on the board . . . the man deserves to be treated better than he is being treated today. To have a man with that kind of experience at your back can only be to the club's good.'

From the floor shareholders asked why White and the Kellys were trying to remove Farrell. White's explanation – that 'I do not agree with him and although he has been asked to resign has decided not to' – was greeted with a cry of 'Shame!'

'We are sitting here tearing ourselves apart,' said Des O'Neill, speaking for a shareholder from Carluke, Lanarkshire. 'We must not forget that we in this room do not own Celtic Football Club. The people all around the world who have Celtic in their hearts own Celtic.'

'I don't see how it is anything other than harsh and oppresive to remove Jimmy Farrell,' said another proxy, Frank McAteer.

'I cannot think of a blacker day,' said Len Murray. 'It seems to me there are three qualities in the conduct of the affairs of Celtic Football Club as I knew it: qualities like decency, honour and integrity. Where on earth are they this afternoon?

' . . . Jimmy Farrell is the guy who succeeds in the tradition of the great Celtic elder statesmen of the past: the Robert Kellys and the Desmond Whites and the Tom Devlins. My God, each of them must be turning in their graves . . . '

With an eye on the coming semi-final and remembering the result after the AGM in October 1990, he told the board sarcastically: 'Let me also commend you in your sense of timing, because that is impeccable. It is the same sort of timing that was displayed in October 1990, remember? What do we say about people who don't learn from experience?'

Low rose to speak. The Chairman, remembering the recorded conversation at the Westerwood hotel, asked: 'You don't have your tape with you? No?'

'No, you tripped over the wires, remember?'

'No, you said that.'

Low proposed an adjournment to allow the directors to 'deal with this matter in a satisfactory manner', but Kelly refused. He then allowed cousin Michael to reply to the attack on him.

Michael Kelly called it a day for 'sadness rather than anger' and refused to trade attacks, instead putting on record Farrell's 'great service' to the club. But he believed Farrell's speech revealed why Kelly and White asked him to resign. 'Jimmy in his speech clearly indicated that there was not . . . unity on the board,' he said.

'Christopher White and myself from October 1990 to the present time worked actively at every single board meeting

to try and heal that breach. And we came a long way because
... since that time ... we have convinced Kevin we have the
good of the club at heart. I think Tom understands that the
only way forward for this club is if a majority of the major
shareholders ... can get their act together and work in a
united and concerted way ... I think this is the last chance
for Celtic and therefore we are asking Jimmy Farrell to leave
the board, in order that we can achieve that unity ... '

Proposals for redeveloping Parkhead or moving to
another site were risky for a club 'of our poor profit record'.
It would require ' fundamental changes' in how the club was
financed, including shareholdings.

But 'Jimmy shouldn't say to Christopher and myself,
"Don't start buying and selling Celtic shares." Because it
wasn't us that started buying and selling Celtic's shares ...
We have never offered them for sale ... We couldn't sell
them at any price! If other people are driving up the value
artificially from £2 or £3 to, I am told, £300, £350, that is not
something that can be laid at our door.'

Shareholders and fans had not had the information they
asked for about Superstadia's proposals because the board
were concerned in case 'we implement any scheme that
causes this club to go under ... We are going into this not
only with our eyes open but after due and cool and
considered examination.' Independent financial and
technical advice was being sought, and the plan was
sufficiently viable for the Glasgow Development Agency to
consider funding a £250,000 feasibility study into the
Cambuslang site.

On the alternate plan by Miller Construction, he said:
'This was not something that I concealed from Jimmy Farrell
or from other directors. This was something that simply
wasn't circulated.'

'By Mr Cassidy?' demanded Farrell.

'Michael, you said it was concealed,' asked a shareholder.
'Who concealed it?'

'I don't know. I don't think it was a question of concealed
in order to hide it from the board. I think it was the position
that there were several options for the development of Celtic
Park under review, and a closing date was fixed for them to
be assessed. The Miller proposal came in late and uninvited,

and it was being kept in a bottom drawer in case all of the others fell flat and it could be resuscitated. There was no intention to hide it from the board.'

Shareholders interrupted. 'You said it was kept in a bottom drawer. Things kept in a bottom drawer are concealed.'

'You have just denied knowledge of its existence, Michael.'

'There is no denial of the knowledge of its existence,' said Kelly, 'because it was one of the many leaks that have come from the highest level of this club. When you talk about bad PR, it is not the PR company that is screwing it up. It is the people leaking stories week in and week out to every single newspaper and radio station. So don't jeer about public relations . . .

'The chief executive had decided that there was to be an option for Cambuslang and that there was to be another option, not the Miller one, for Celtic Park. That is a management decision . . . There is therefore nothing devious or surreptitious about a report lying in someone's drawer waiting for the appropiate moment to be brought out . . . '

He accused Len Murray of making a 'rather cheap' point about the timing of the meeting. 'Since January we have been hounded and harried and threatened that EGMs will come up this time or that time or at the end of the season . . . It was an intolerable situation for the board to try and operate the business of the club with that threat hanging over us. Action had to be taken to resolve that, and that is what we did. 'The 1990 AGM had been fixed so long in advance and its falling just before the Skol Cup final was an 'unfortunate coincidence'.

He added: 'If Len Murray is suggesting that the performance of the team had been affected by this call to the EGM then he is not coming to the games the way I am . . . Don't try and dramatise it in the terms that the team will win or lose tomorrow on the basis of our having a meeting today. The team is on a huge unbeaten run.'

On a show of hands the resolution to remove Farrell was lost by 17 votes to 32. Chris White, in the name of himself, Miss Kelly, Mrs Adele Daly, Michael Kelly and Francis McCrossan, again called for a poll vote, to a cry of 'Shame! Judas!' from the floor.

It was 4.30 p.m. Kevin Kelly suggested adjourning until 6.30 p.m. to allow the scrutineers to work their way through the count, complicated by the number of disqualified votes to subtract. In fact the meeting did not resume for nearly five hours.

Chapter Nine

WHEN REBELS
FALL OUT

I

We had achieved 12 straight wins when we played Rangers in the Scottish Cup semi-final at Hampden on 31 March. Some of you may recall there had been a 'low-key' EGM the night before! Lashing rain and gale-force winds made the playing conditions at Hampden that night extremely difficult for both teams.

We needlessly conceded a goal on the stroke of half-time and that mistake ultimately cost us the game. We pounded the goal in the second half but we didn't enjoy any luck. The final minutes of the game saw us denied a certain penalty. It was a bitter disappointment as I felt the team's play had progressed tremendously up till then.

– Liam Brady

THE rebels adjourned to Dempsey's office. They were optimistic but not certain of victory, except for Low who was already sporting a large cigar, so he went to work with a calculator, running through the estimates again.

The EGM did not resume until 9.21 p.m. The chief scrutineer had to read out eight paragraphs of provisions concerning specific shareholders and proxies whose votes had been allowed or disqualified before he reached the results.

David Smith's appointment to the board was approved by 869 votes to 569. Tom Grant's removal was defeated by 1,424 votes to nil. Finally, Resolution 3, to remove James Matthew Farrell. For: 681. Against: 745.

The Jock Stein lounge exploded into cheers. Farrell held his arms aloft like a heavyweight who had just retained his title, and in a real sense that is what he was. He was 70 years old and the battle had been exhausting, but he had emerged a winner. The shareholders started singing: 'For he's a jolly good fellow . . . ' Low walked down to the front to shake his hand, combining an affectionate gesture to Farrell with a dig at Smith, White and Kelly. The EGM result was 2-1 to the rebels. Unfortunately the Celtic team did not fare so well the next night.

For shareholders and supporters alike that meeting was a turning point. The rebels had until then been viewed publicly with a mixture of hopeful encouragement by their supporters and worried disdain by their opponents. Now they were a force to be reckoned with. The board could no longer rule as they pleased. The balance of power had changed, and everybody knew it.

It showed too that Route One to Goal – going the way of gathering shareholder support and pushing for seats on the board – could be a viable way to go. McCann felt the same euphoria that night. He was still keen on Celtic's Future plc but he could see what Route One offered. He had the money and the business skills. Brian Dempsey had the fans' support and the political skills. Low had the technical knowledge and tactical skills. It would take a coalition of the Dempsey and McCann teams to win.

The board had already accepted Superstadia's recommendation of Cambuslang as the preferred option, subject to it being proven financially viable. In April they went public with it. The announcement had all the PR accessories Celtic could afford, glossy artist's impressions of the finished structure looking like an American Superbowl stadium. It would have everything: 52,000 seats in two tiers, a 200-bedroom hotel, leisure and sports facilities, a permanent stage with a mobile acoustic curtain which could close off up to 15,000 of the seats. Alongside it would be a 'retail village', an eight screen cinema complex, a 30-lane bowling alley, drive-in fastfood restaurants, two railway stations and parking for 4,500 cars. The cost of the whole development would be £100-£120 million but, said the board, the first phase of two touchline stands holding 32,000 spectators would cost 'only' £30 million. The rest could be built as income came in from the commercial developments. The annual interest charges alone on the borrowing needed to pay for it all would be £3 million.

The projected figures for the income were wildly optimistic. The Superstadia consultant Professor Gwyn Kennedy admitted that the hotel within the stadium was important to the economics of the plan, but the Glasgow hotel market was becoming crowded with the Hilton chain about to open the city's first five-star hotel right next door to the existing Holiday Inn.

Superstadia's projection of average attendances at Celtic games was 30,000 in spite of proposed ticket prices which were 40 per cent higher. Yet later that month the crowd at Parkhead to watch Celtic's 2-0 win over Dunfermline was only 12,649. 'We reckon on an increase in attendance of 4,500 considering the new facility,' said Professor Kennedy, but that would still not reach the board's average figure of 30,000.

Football was intended to bring in only a third of the football stadium's income but the projections for American football matches, rugby, boxing and rock concerts were equally over-optimistic. A separate stadium company, with Celtic as a minority shareholder, would own the stadium.

Fergus McCann, before he left for Canada two weeks later, described it as a 'PR exercise' which consisted of a 'house of cards to be financed by the fairy godmother'. He added: 'The present management have neither the abilities nor the backing of the supporters, let alone credibility in the business community to arrest the club's decline, and they have no equity capital on which to base *any* construction plan.'

Perhaps the best description of the plan came in a *Herald* headline which called Cambuslang Celtic's 'field of dreams'. It was the title of a Kevin Costner film in which the hero builds a baseball stadium in the middle of a prairie for a group of ghosts. It was a prophetic headline: no one but ghosts or imaginary teams would play professional football there.

The board might also have read the writing on the road. On one route to Cambuslang the name is abbreviated so it can be written on the road to direct drivers. The abbreviation is C'lang!

II

UNFORTUNATELY around this time the rebels themselves were split. Their advisors continued to meet to discuss Celtic's Future plc. It would be difficult to float a company whose only object was to take over another company. Celtic's lawyers could tie it up in legal disputes over Stock Exchange procedures or Takeover Panel rules or the Celtic board might try to buy shares and disrupt it from within. The new company would then have to push through a hostile takeover bid which would need to be agreed by a 75 per cent majority of Celtic shareholders. In contrast, putting directors on the board needed only a simple majority and authorising an increase in share capital needed a two-thirds majority.

But one of the biggest problems would have been persuading fans to put money into a company other than The Celtic Football and Athletic Company Ltd, especially if there was no guarantee it could take over the club. Even if they did it would be difficult to maintain their support if the company became bogged down in legal and technical wrangling.

Finally on 26 April the Dempsey-Keanes team met at the Royal Scot Hotel on the main western approach road into Edinburgh. Along with Dempsey, Low and John and Dominic Keane was Sandy Moffat. Low and Moffat concluded that the Celtic's Future plan would not work. They would follow Route One to Goal and would try to persuade Fergus to go along with them.

Three days later at PKF's offices in Glasgow there was a crunch meeting of the two teams. The Canadian had invested time, money and effort in his plan and in other circumstances it could have worked. But Britain was a more regulated market than Bermuda or even Canada and they faced a board that was clinging to power tenaciously. McCann's lawyer had been in touch with The Takeover Panel who had said that although a private limited company, Celtic was of sufficient public interest for their takeover rules to apply.

The meeting became heated. Somebody suggested there was a problem raising the money.

John Keane was a quiet man and probably as wealthy as McCann. He was quick to respond to this. He threw down a qualified Banker's draft and said: 'There's my bloody money!' When the meeting broke up, so did the best hope of Celtic's Future plc taking off.

McCann's public relations company, Charles Barker Scotland, put out a Press release on the day Fergus returned to Canada feeling deeply let down. He had now cancelled plans to invest £7.2 million of his own money to 'kick-start' an injection of £17 million in capital into Celtic.

'I am naturally extremely disappointed that after a great deal of work by many people, a lot of planning and many meetings on both sides of the Atlantic over the last 18 months, my plan has not been realised,' he said. 'However, this week the commitments which I had received from other lead investors for most of the £5 million required have now been withdrawn.'

The two teams split and the ill-feeling briefly spilled over into disagreements about who should pay what fees for which work by whose advisors. After the euphoria of the EGM only a month before, the sense of disappointment was all the greater. But the rebel faction was always a coalition, never a consortium, and a fragile one at that. It was made up of strong personalities and egos bound together by feelings for an institution that was as much an idea and a cause as a mere football club. The coalition remained fragile even after they ceased to be rebels and became the new government of Celtic.

The pace had been relentless now for a long time. The last six months had provided an emotional roller-coaster ride: the gradual build-up of excitement as their support among shareholders grew, the explosion of media attention, the demand for seats on the board, the arrival of a corporate specialist to oppose them, the trial of strength they had won to save two directors and the split of the two teams in the coalition. They were all in need of break. Batteries needed recharging. It was time for a holiday.

III

LIKE three musketeers Dempsey, Low and John Keane set off on a light-hearted escapade to let their hair down, have fun and relax. They decided to take up an invitation to visit Eddy Keane in Bermuda. After months of long days of meetings, faxes and phone calls, Keane and Low relaxed on the plane to New York with a few drinks. Dempsey was not a drinker. They arrived at the Marriott Hotel, overlooking Times Square, tired and jet-lagged but set off almost immediately for a meal in Little Italy.

Wine was taken with the meal and when they returned to the hotel they retired to the cocktail bar. The bar revolved very slowly to reveal the view of Times Square but no one mentioned this to Low. One minute he was talking to Dempsey, aware of a hugh neon sign for Sony over Dempsey's shoulder. Then he turned to Keane and there was the Sony sign over his shoulder. He turned back to Dempsey, only now there was a Fujitsu sign behind him. 'Christ!' he thought. 'I'm hallucinating. I think I'd better get to bed.'

Next day they indulged themselves by hiring a black stretch limousine to tour the sights of New York, from the Empire State Building to Chinatown, with Low in the back snapping away with a camera. Only afterwards did he discover there was no film in the camera. They took high tea at Trump Plaza. Jim Doherty flew down from Toronto to join them for an evening before they left for Hamilton, Bermuda.

On the island they checked into the Princess Hotel, which was managed by a client of Low's, and then went down to Flanagan's Bar which is owned by Eddy Keane. You could not miss the bar – it sported the biggest Tricolour on the island. Keane had had a battle on his hands to open an Irish bar in the stoutly British Bermuda, especially on the best site in Front Street in the capital. The Bermuda establishment had tried to block him at every turn. When the bar finally opened, Keane bought the biggest green-white-and-gold he could find. 'That really pissed 'em all off,' he said.

Keane had one of the biggest houses overlooking the best golf course in Bermuda, worth about $6 million, with a clear view of the 18th tee. Like the bar it was full of Irish and republican memorabilia. Some years ago President Ronald Reagan and Prime Minister Margaret Thatcher's husband, Denis, were due to play a round of golf on the course. The US Secret Service checked out all the houses with a clear view and had a fright when they saw all of Keane's souvenirs. 'They did everything but fucking body-search me,' he said. When the famous men did play their game the next day, two lookalikes preceded them around the course.

Dempsey had to leave a day early when a relative fell ill. Keane and Low were to fly back to Glasgow next day via Boston. They had several hours to kill there so they decided to have a pint in Boston's most famous Irish pubs. They had a couple in the Black Rose, which is lined with pictures of Republican heroes, and a couple more in the Purple Shamrock. By the time they reached the airport again they had forgotten where they had put their luggage and nearly missed the plane. They finally made it into their first-class seats and Low accepted a glass of the complementary champagne.

Suddenly he heard: 'Mr Low! Mr Low!' It was the stewardess trying to wake him up. He was back in Glasgow, having slept all the way.

IV

THE holiday was over. It was back to business. The Takeover Panel had already been consulted about Celtic's Future plc and the rebels had reason to believe the Panel's rules would apply to Celtic in the event of a takeover by a public company. But could they apply without a takeover?

Panel rules were designed to protect shareholders of public companies but they could also apply to private limited companies such as Celtic if it was in the public interest. Owning 30 per cent of a company was frequently enough to control it. So one rule was that no individual, company or group of individuals acting together – known as 'concerted persons' – could control 30 per cent or more of

121

a company without giving the remaining shareholders a chance to sell out at the best price.

If the rules were applied to Celtic, the members of the voting pact would be classed as 'concerted persons'. Since between them they owned more than 30 per cent of the shares, they would have to offer to buy all the shares at the highest price that had been paid in the last 12 months. The price was £300 a share, and the pact could simply not afford to do that.

Every opportunity to turn the rebels' substantial minority into a majority had to be explored. They considered making another offer for Adele Daly's 1,132 shares. They believed she was willing to sell at least some of them but had been convinced by her nephew, Chris White, and David Smith not to.

Another possibility arose with Kevin Kelly's shareholding. The late Sir Robert Kelly had been a large shareholder and he left all his shares to his wife. Lady Kelly also had shares in her own right. She died in 1991 and all the shares she had inherited would go to Kevin, Sir Robert's nephew, but her own shares went to a Mr James Swift, one of two executors of her estate. The shares were still registered in the names of the executors. Low was looking for a way to get control of, or at least neutralise, those shares, which were still outside the pact.

Wills are public documents and he obtained a copy of Lady Kelly's from Hamilton Sheriff Court. The will contained a number of codicils, or amendments, she had made to her first version of it. Two of these laid down that none of her property was to be left to any member of the Kelly family, whom she had not always got along with. The first amendment was in the form of a note to a Mrs Cecily Aitken who was to share the rest of the estate with Swift, apart from as few bequests to priests and Lady Kelly's niece, Maureen Reilly. The note read:

Cecily,
There are two boxes of jewellery and one gold European Cup in the vaults of the Bank of Scotland, Burnside Branch, and if you do not want to give Maureen Reilly who is in my will the piece of jewellery I at one time wished her to have,

do not trouble and ignore the request in my will.
If you consider any member of the Kelly family should get
any piece of jewellery with Kelly connection please give it to
whoever it may be, but nothing more.

Lady Kelly

In the second, she insisted nothing of my estate should be transferred 'to any member of the Kelly family'. The second amendment could mean that none of her Celtic shares – not just those she had in her own right, but also those left to her by Sir Robert – should pass to a Kelly. The rebels made an offer to Swift and Mrs Aitken to show them how valuable the shares were. The object was to persuade them it was worth fighting a court case, if necessary, to ensure that all the shares passed to them and not Kevin Kelly. The offer was put at a total figure of nearly half a million pounds. Any dispute would tie up the shares and keep them out of the pact's control. Swift later sold 100 shares to David Smith but claimed it took 13 weeks to receive payment, which pushed him in the direction of the rebels. Swift subsequently sold 164 shares to Gerald Weisfeld.

Weisfeld and his stepson Michael McDonald were expressing an interest in becoming involved to James Dempsey, Brian's cousin and financial director. McDonald was a real Celtic fan and the Weisfeld Partnership was already an executive box holder.

The 25th anniversary of Celtic's winning of the European Cup was in May. The rebels took a table at the Lisbon Lions dinner on the 24th but the gloss was taken off the anniversary for the club by their mishandling of the situation. Four Lisbon Lions who had been taken on to help with hospitality had felt aggrieved that the arrangement was terminated by Cassidy. There was a dispute over the commemorative video and two different versions were marketed: the official one backed by the board, and the one backed by the Lisbon Lions.

Low was told to requisition another EGM. This meeting would introduce one share, one vote, instead of one vote to every ten shares, and issue £2.3 million worth of shares to existing shareholders in proportion to their holdings, £2.1 million worth of shares to Dempsey, John Keane and Eddy

Keane, and £600,000 worth of shares to executive box club holders in payment of the money they had already loaned to the club.

But the requisition was withdrawn after a meeting between Low and Moffat for the rebels and Kevin Sweeney and Elspeth Campbell of McGrigor Donald for the board, when they were told the board would be putting forward their own proposals. It was time, instead, to concentrate on buying more shares. That meant back to Ireland and some tough negotiating in a cowshed.

Chapter Ten

A MORTGAGE ON PARADISE

So far this season we have played 22 league matches and
lost only three, and in the matches against Hibernian, Partick
Thistle and Rangers, which we lost, on the balance of play I
would argue we deserved to win. In fact, with the exception
of Aberdeen in the first half at Celtic Park against us earlier
this month no one has really outplayed us.

– Liam Brady

DEALS are about people and you have to accept people as
and where you find them: in their luxury apartments or their
council flats, in expensive hotel suites or modest milking
parlours. One measure of the range of support for Celtic was
the variety of places in which you found their shareholders.
By the summer of 1992 shares were being bought in smaller
batches, and they were being found in more out of the way
places, including the bandit country of South Fermanagh.

Low flew to Belfast Aldergrove airport and was picked up
by Aidan Neeson. They had to drive to the home of the
particular shareholder they had gone to meet because he
had no phone. In this area two men in suits in a black BMW
driving uninvited up to a farmhouse out of sight of
neighbours would not usually be good news. They knocked
on the door and waited. No answer, but off to the right a
curtain moved.

They decided to go for lunch in Enniskillen. In the afternoon they returned to the farmhouse. A ruddy-faced man in black overalls and Wellingtons appeared from round the corner of the house.

'Good afternoon. I'm Mr Low. I've come to make you an offer for your Celtic Football Club shares.' The man looked at him suspiciously. 'Could I come in to discuss it?'

'Come in here.' They followed him into a cowshed. 'Sit down there.' He motioned to a group of milk urns. The trio sat down to talk.

It was to be a lengthy conversation. Low was wearing a £500 tailor-made suit which would have made him look at home on any share-dealing floor in any stockbrokers' office in the world. It had not been made for cowsheds. But share dealing is share dealing wherever you do it. 'Like I said, I would like to buy your shares in Celtic Football Club.'

The farmer's father had gone to Glasgow as a young man to make his money, and while there he had acquired shares in Celtic. 'I could never sell those shares,' he said. 'They have been in the family for 60 years.'

Low began to explain what was happening back in Glasgow but sensed that the man was not paying close attention to it. This man was more likely to be a seller than an active supporter of the rebel cause. He reverted to the subject of an offer for the shares. 'No, no,' said the man. 'They're precious to me. I could never sell those shares.'

The conversation moved backwards and forwards between the two men in turn. 'No, no,' said the man yet again. Then he suddenly added: 'But if you upped it by £1,000 I would have to deal there!'

Back in Glasgow the board were embarking on a deal of their own. They joined with Rangers, Aberdeen, Dundee United and Hearts to give the Scottish Football League notice that they intended to resign and form their own Scottish Super League. It was the culmination of years of frustration by the largest clubs with a league set-up designed to help smaller clubs milk their loyal support. A visit by Rangers or Celtic had meant a bumper cash pay-out for any club they played, though now Rangers had become the jackpot prize. But with their growing European ambitions the existing league arrangement was beginning to look to Rangers more and more like a series of charity games.

David Murray companies handled the feasibility study and the public relations. Part of the plan for the new league was for voting rights and commercial income from the Super League to be based on performance. Admission to the league would also require 'appropriate' stadium and financial standards. Celtic joined in the plan but Kevin Kelly's attitude to it appeared ambivalent at best. Eventually the threat of a breakaway was enough to win David Murray most of what he wanted from the existing league.

Celtic's own commercial income was hardly improving. They launched The Celtic Family, a card discount scheme which offered Celtic supporters savings on a range of goods from new cars to furniture to foreign holidays. As part of the launch promotion Lisbon Lion Bobby Lennox and world champion boxer Pat Clinton were presented with the first and second green and gold cards. There was also a new Celtic mail order catalogue. It was an attempt to move in the right direction but the start-up costs were out of all proportion to the returns for Celtic. The offered savings failed to attract sufficient card-holders. But the sale of Celtic products was generating only half as much as Rangers earned from theirs.

The team's only trophy that year was the Challenger Cup they lifted after drubbing Manchester City 3-1 in Dublin. Manager Liam Brady went shopping again, bringing in Andy Payton from Middlesbrough and dispatching Chris Morris and Derek Whyte to the same club in return at a speed which surprised the two players. He also gave West Ham £1.5 million for Stuart Slater. Until then the running story of the year had been the 'Will he? Won't he?' saga of whether or not terms could be reached to persuade captain Paul McStay to continue his career at Parkhead.

In spite of Bobby Lennox's role in promoting The Celtic Family, relations with the Lisbon Lions continued to deteriorate. As well as Jim Craig's alliance with the rebels, the pride of the Lions was hurt. They eventually refused to appear before a pre-season friendly at Parkhead against Manchester United. Billy McNeill accused the club of paying 'scant attention' to their achievements in the anniversary year. The strain in the relationship had begun when Celtic had turned down their request for a testimonial match. Kevin Kelly dismissed a testimonial 25 years after the event as 'nonsense' and insisted that the SFA and Scottish League would not countenance it. Yet the whole year was turning into a lost opportunity for both the club and their ex-players almost on a scale of the original triumph.

Cassidy was still talking a good game, promising that Celtic would go into the financial services market with a new Celtic credit card to be issued in association with either Access or Visa, which would give the club payments based on the number of transactions by cardholders.

But he was removed in October after less than two years of his original three-year contract had run. His failure to stop speaking out even when instructed not to proved too much even for the faction on the board which had appointed him. They could not agree severance terms and later Cassidy sued for breach of contract leading to an embarrassing court case for both sides.

A deal was reached with Glasgow Development Agency to pay £2 million for the land at Cambuslang, but only after planning permission had been granted. In May Superstadia had been given the job of handling the planning application and finding the funding for the stadium. For this they were to be paid £1.5 million plus expenses of £250,000. The fee would be deferred until the funding was found but Celtic agreed to pay £500,000 up front. The GDA agreed to pay half of that and the £250,000 was handed over in December. Accountants Ernst & Young were appointed to act as independent project managers on the club's behalf.

Superstadia, with David Smith's agreement, subcontracted the job of finding the funding to Patrick Nally of StadiVarius, the small consultancy based in Oxford, but his fee was not included in the fee already agreed with Superstadia. He suggested that possible funding packages could mean Celtic would have a stadium for nothing more than the £2 million they would pay for the land.

Stories kept appearing about the level of contamination on the Cambuslang site. It was polluted with toxic waste from former steelworks which had seeped into old mineworkings but the cost of cleaning up the land had not been established. Some accounts painted lurid pictures of any stadium toppling into pools of toxins in old mine-shafts, but the key point was that Celtic would have to prove to the planning authorities that the land was safe.

One small increase in commercial income that year came from . . . Brian Dempsey. He had withdrawn from the four executive boxes he and his companies had at Parkhead, and which had cost him £100,000 a year, but he agreed to take one box again.

That year Celtic's annual general meeting was later than usual, coming only nine days before Christmas. Some seasonal goodwill managed to seep into the besieged board and Michael Kelly, who had spoken so strongly for Jimmy Farrell's dismissal only nine months before now proposed him for re-election.

But goodwill did not mean going soft and David Smith, who responded to all the financial questions, underwent a sustained grilling at the hands of the well-prepared rebel financial team. At the previous year's AGM there had been 16 shareholders or their proxies; this year there were 68. Chairman Kevin Kelly was careful not to allow one or two speakers 'to hog the whole meeting' but for a while it seemed that every speaker he called was not only in the rebel camp but was financially or legally trained: Low, corporate advisor Derek Douglas, accountant Paul McNeill, businessman Brian Dempsey, solicitor Len Murray, banker-turned-businessman Dominic Keane, solicitor Marco Guarino.

One after another they quizzed Smith in detail on the accounts, drawing out information, putting follow-up questions, analysing his answers. Never had Celtic's finances been so rigorously examined. And with good reason.

Smith reported an operating loss of just over £960,000 for the 12 months to the end of June, compared with a profit of more than £1.2 million the previous year. But the total loss topped £2.6 million, because Smith had split the trading loss from losses made on the transfer market. It was right to give a separate figure for operating the week-to-week business of the club, but transfers – trading places – were also a regular part of the club's business. The amount owed to trade creditors grew by nearly £600,000, from £320,000 to £900,000, taking the loss on the year to £3.2 million.

There had been a disappointing season on the pitch, depressing attendances, 2,000 seats had been unavailable and an increased number of staff had been employed, including ten more on the playing staff to take the total to 58. 'Speculative' costs had increased. There were the thousands spent on projects that had not delivered the return expected, such as the £250,000 spent on the Celtic Family scheme.

Buying players cost the club £1.7 million more than it received from selling them in 1991-92 and in the first part of 1992-93 cost £750,000. Borrowings rose to £4.9 million. Smith insisted this was 'comfortably' within the overdraft facility agreed with the Bank but refused to reveal the amount of the facility.

Dempsey pointed out that interest on a £5 million overdraft must be about £100,000 a quarter so that if nothing else happened before June the next year the overdraft would rise to £5.3 million. 'Are you still feeling comfortable within your facility?'

'I am still comfortable at the level within the facility, yes.'

'But you are not far within the facility, are you?'

'I am comfortable within the facility that is available at the present time.'

'I think you have to come a bit cleaner here, Mr Smith. You are getting close to the mark.'

'I don't think so . . .'

'Can you tell us what the existing facility is?'

'No, I don't think we will disclose that at this time.'

When Dempsey asked about the current financial year, Smith replied: 'I am happy we will get to the end of the current financial year . . .'

'I'm not sure I like your choice of words. You are saying you are confident the company will get to the end of the financial year?'

'Yes'.

'You are not giving me a lot of confidence that you will get there with ease . . . Can we have peace of mind from you tonight that we will get there adequately, satisfactorily and without danger to Celtic Football Club?'

'I expect to have peace of mind myself, and if I can convey that to the shareholders I will be very happy.'

'I am not convinced but I honestly hope you are right.'

Dominic Keane wanted to know if the Bank of Scotland had put any conditions on Celtic running up a £5 million overdraft. He had been a banker for 20 years, working in the corporate department of a branch in Glasgow dealing with large Scottish, UK and international companies. It struck him as odd that a bank would let any company of Celtic's size run up a debt of £5 million without some conditions, such as asking the directors to give personal guarantees or insisting on an increase in the share capital to bring in more cash.

If an ordinary man takes out a mortgage or a home improvement loan, the bank takes a security over the house. If he fails to repay the loan, it can take the house and re-sell it to get its money back. With a company, the bank can take a security over the company buildings or it can ask the directors to sign personal guarantees: they have to guarantee the loan and all their property is then at risk, including their houses.

Smith told him the Bank had not asked for any guarantee from the directors. 'It is a matter which has never been raised, other than apparently in the Press,' he said sarcastically. 'It is not a matter of discussion between the board or any individual director and the Bank.'

Keane was not so easily fobbed off. 'The Bank of Scotland has no security whatsoever for £5 million of borrowings by the club? Is that correct? They have no security, they have never raised the question of security?'

'Could I answer the question first that you asked? The Bank have not at any time sought any personal guarantees of any kind from any director.'

'I accept that.'

'The Bank have security over the ground or the buildings at Celtic Park.' In effect, Parkhead had been mortgaged, and the accounts did not mention it.

'I don't think that is stated in the accounts.'

'I think I am right in saying that the Bank did not have security at the date of the accounts.'

A major event like giving a bank security over your property should be noted in the accounts, even if it happens after the end of the financial year, said Keane.

Smith's reply was odd, to say the least. 'I am not at all certain that they have security now.'

'Could somebody on the board please tell me if the Bank of Scotland have security for the borrowings?'

'The Bank have security over the ground.'

'When?'

'The Bank obtained that recently. I cannot give you the precise date.'

'Does that mean that there has been some concern expressed by the Bank, in spite of the very comfortable relationship you were talking about?'

'Of course there is.'

'Why not admit that this company is in severe financial difficulties and then we will all rally and support it, instead of sitting there accepting everything in the garden is rosy?'

'I don't think anyone here is saying everything in the garden is rosy. I have said quite specifically the opposite . . .'

'With respect, are you saying as Vice-Chairman you are not aware whether the security had been granted or not? I find that astonishing!'

'I was unaware, and indeed I am standing here unaware, if the legalities have been completed at this point in time. That is the simple fact.'

Solicitor Marco Guarino, a proxy for James Magill of County Tyrone, took up the torch and quizzed Smith on the implications of mortgaging the ground. Between questions Smith had confirmed that security was about to be granted over Parkhead but the paperwork had not yet been completed.

'When did discussions take place regarding the granting of that security?' asked Guarino.

'Over a period of time – I mean years – this matter has been referred to by the company's bankers. Indeed I can say that the first time I spoke to the company's bankers it was one of the first items they raised, and they said they had raised it on numerous occasions in previous years.'

'In the past when the Bank had wanted it as security the board were not prepared to grant it?'

'I cannot speak for the board previously, but one way or another security was not granted.'

'I take it you will be aware of the implications if the Bank decided to call that security?'

'I am equally aware of the implications at any time if it calls in its lending.'

'If . . . in June 1993 . . . we have a further deficit of the magnitude of 1991-92 and that goes beyond the facility the Bank has extended presently to the club, are you able to tell us what the Bank has indicated they will do in that event?'

'It has not been a matter that has been discussed with the Bank.'

'Are you saying it has never been discussed or even thought about that the facility might be exceeded and the Bank might decide "Enough is enough". . . If that facility is exceeded what do the board anticipate that the Bank will do?'

'I have absolutely no idea. As far as I am concerned that is a hypothetical question.'

'It is a valid question.'

'It is a valid question, yes . . .'

'If, for example, the Bank decided to call in the security they could sell the ground, could they not?'

'I doubt they would take that step.'

'Would you agree with me it would be open for them to do that?'

'It would be open for them to do that.'

'What would become of the team with regard to playing then?'

In other circumstances Smith's answer might have been humorous. Instead of telling Guarino he was speculating or asking hypothetical questions, he said: 'I think you are moving into the ground of hypothesis.' Grady was more worried about what ground Celtic would move into if Parkhead ever had to be sold off.

The board were repeatedly asked who was taking responsibility for the £3.2 million loss. The answer was that the board were collectively responsible, and by the time the directors' fees of £2,500 each were discussed the seasonal spirit had all but gone.

'Would it not be the right and proper thing to do, particularly in the light of the serious financial position of this company, that the directors should waive any remuneration which they obtained during this crisis period?' asked financial analyst Derek Douglas. 'Mr Chairman, I move that the directors should re-examine the benefits which they obtain from the company and . . . rather than take money from the company, consider putting money into the company during this difficult period, as so many of the supporters do on a week-to-week basis . . .'

Chris White revealed that the total payments to Kevin Kelly were between £5,000 and £10,000, Jack McGinn earned between £35,000 to £40,000 and the two executive directors, stadium manager Tom Grant and the company secretary £40,000 to £45,000 including benefits in kind but not pension contributions. He refused to disclose how much Michael Kelly Associates earned as the club's public relations firm.

At Dempsey's instigation a motion that the directors should go without their £2,500 fees was withdrawn, and the spirit of goodwill returned. Michael Kelly proposed the re-election of Farrell as director, seconded by Grant. Farrell thanked them and the people who spoke for him at the EGM 'which is the reason I am up for re-election in the first place'. Kevin Kelly was also re-elected.

The meeting ended with manager Liam Brady reviewing the season on the field. 'Rest assured that I have prepared this myself, and it has not come from Michael Kelly Associates,' he began.

The semi-final defeat by Rangers was 'a bitter disappointment, as I felt the team's play had progressed tremendously up till then'. The crucial period over Christmas would bring games against Hearts, Dundee United and, of course, Rangers, but 'so far this season the team has not played to its full potential'. Wins would put Celtic back in the championship race.

'With regard to the cup competitions that we have been involved in this season, the Skol Cup semi-final defeat at the hands of Aberdeen was disappointing on an occasion when our performance did not come up to the standard we had set. The games did seem to come at the worst possible time, with defeats by Hibernian and Cologne in the weeks leading up to it being damaging to confidence and morale.

'In addition, we entered the game without Tony Mowbray, out through suspension, and the fact that the goal which settled the issue in Aberdeen's favour came from a corner kick perhaps tells its own story as to how much Tony's commanding aerial presence was missed.'

Europe was a very different story and there should be no shame over Celtic's efforts in the UEFA Cup. Borussia Dortmund had been a superior side, whose class and experience eventually told at Parkhead. But Celtic had matched them for over half an hour in the second-round tie. 'Who knows how matters would have resolved themselves in that particular game against Dortmund had we scored a crucial goal in the first half,' he said. 'Neither should it be forgotten that we eliminated a Bundesliga side called Cologne, and our tremendous 3-0 second-leg victory showed the ability to mix passion and commitment with skill to win through in style.'

He had a first-team squad of 21, at least three of whom could be sold to generate cash and cut the wage bill, but they would not be the most valuable ones. He had bought in seven new first team players and sold seven, at an overall net cost of £2 million.

Brady ended with an appeal for unity. 'The way forward for this club is to maintain a strong, united front and in this respect I appeal to all Celtic-minded people to pull as one.

'It is important in this day and age to have freedom of speech but if we could do away with the seemingly constant public wranglings between different groups of Celtic-minded people I believe it would allow our ambitions to be fully concentrated on on-the-field matters. A daily diet of in-fighting, for want of a better phrase, in the voracious media does nobody any good at all.'

For a while his plea was heeded. The EGM which the voting pact directors had called to remove two directors had passed with the board still intact. The 'master of the gratuitous insult', Terry Cassidy, had gone. Peace at Parkhead and goodwill for all fans seemed almost as close as Christmas itself. But peace can last only if it has a fair and financially sound base, and that was missing at Celtic.

Chapter Eleven

THE CALL TO ARMS

BY the beginning of 1993 it looked as if the Celtic team and the rebels had each hit a brick wall. The most despairing feared the New Year 1-0 defeat at Rangers' hands might become as much of a seasonal event as first-footing. A week later a 0-0 draw with Clyde made them the first ever Celtic team not to score in five games on the run.

The rebels seemed pinned at controlling around 40 per cent of the shareholding and could not break through to a majority. They had fallen out with their biggest potential investor who had publicly announced the split and withdrawn to Montreal. Michael Kelly and David Smith had called on McCann in Montreal. They said they were there to assure him that they saw him as 'a friendly potential source of capital for the club,' he said later. Things, they said, had changed since his earlier approaches to other directors to provide investment and management skills had been rejected. He was the person they were most likely to approach for money. 'They respected the business success that I had achieved in other fields and also my strong interest in Celtic, and wished to maintain contact with me.'

They also wished to see the McCann-Dempsey split continue. Meanwhile three-quarters of the board were locked into a legally binding pact and were adamantly pursuing plans for a multi-million pound stadium development. Tom Grant, Kevin Kelly and even Liam Brady had called for a period of peace and unity. The momentum seemed to have been lost. Nothing more could be done.

But the situation was unstable. The board were chasing the financial equivalent of an escape trick found only in comics: 'With one bound, the hero was free . . .' The financial situation remained bad. They had hired and fired a chief executive, steamrollered through the appointment of a deputy Chairman and were losing the loyalty of their customers on which the whole company depended. Now they were pinning their hopes on a property development that was hugely more speculative than one they had rejected three years ago, before their overdraft had ballooned to hazardous proportions.

The rebels could not walk away from such a situation, and they had no intentions of doing so. The first priority was to keep their own base secure. Gerald Weisfeld was becoming increasingly interested in the club. It was not impossible that the board would approach him, both as a source of investment and as a way to deny his support to the rebels. So Dempsey and Low acted first. Dempsey sold most of his shares to Weisfeld, making Gerald the largest individual shareholder with about ten per cent. Dempsey, John Keane and Low had spent nearly £500,000 on shares. The money from Weisfeld could go to buy more.

Shares were being acquired as they became available, mainly small parcels, although just before Easter they bought 200, another one per cent stake. David Smith was competing for these shares. All the time the existing shareholders had to be kept informed and encouraged. Dempsey and Low had no intention of repeating the board's mistake of neglecting them. The bigger the team, the more time and effort was required to keep it together.

It was difficult for many shareholders to understand what was going on, especially when the story dropped out of the headlines. Many were, understandably, impatient. But it was important to keep your eyes on the goal. If one path was blocked you had to consider whether to push through or go round it.

Eventually it was decided to form a Celtic Shareholders' Association to represent minority shareholders. Unlike

White and Kelly's Shareholders' Trust, this was not a legally binding pact but a voluntary coming together of individuals, along the lines of a supporters' club. The committee consisted of Bill Gallacher, Peter Maley and Dr Hugh Drake, all direct descendants of Celtic's early greats, on or off the field. The Association's constitution was based on one for a similar association of Hibs' shareholders, just as the founding of Celtic Football Club had been inspired by the success of Hibernian Football Club.

Michael Kelly was asked by Archie MacPherson in a radio interview whether, if the right people came along with £20 million, he would take it. Kelly said he would. McCann, who was still receiving radio and TV transcripts and Press cuttings in Montreal, took Kelly at his word and put together a £21 million package: £12.5 million was either put on a deposit or formally committed. The weight of that investment was meant to generate further investment from the fans and improved loan facilities from the Bank. He faxed Kelly with the news, requesting that he endorse a recapitalisation. 'With the deadlines facing Celtic it is important that we work together on this immediately,' he said.

Kelly expressed interest but asked that any contact between them be kept confidential. McCann pressed for an answer: subject to the details, did Kelly favour accepting the offer of new capital or not? Kelly consulted David Smith who phoned McCann and spoke to him for more than half an hour. Essentially Kelly's answer was that McCann's offer was the same as the plan he announced the previous year which had 'unrealistic' conditions attached to it, but he should really put a detailed proposal to the board.

McCann was furious. The offer was not the same, there were no unrealistic conditions, but all he wanted right then was an affirmative answer from Kelly so that they could move to a meeting. The story of McCann's offer leaked to the Press and Kelly responded by demanding to see what money was on offer. Fergus asked point-blank if Kelly believed McCann was suitable for Celtic and if he would accept the £21 million in principal. Eventually he set a 24-hour deadline for Kelly to give a straight answer.

When Kelly did not meet the deadline, McCann told Pannell Kerr Forster to approach Kevin Kelly, but his answer was the same as his cousin's: put a detailed proposal to the board. The two rebel teams made contact again for the first time since their acrimonious split the previous year. The advisors, Sandy Moffat and Low, met at PKF's offices. The first meeting was very cold. Both sides were cautious. Low tried to act as a broker to bring the two factions together again because, whatever their arguments had been, the two sides needed each other.

'What do you want?' McCann kept asking, as direct as ever. 'What do these guys want?' What he wanted was a commitment in writing. That was agreed and the leaders of the two teams finally met. Brian Dempsey, John Keane and Eddy Keane were prepared to invest £1 million each. So was Albert Friedberg, a highly experienced Toronto-based commodity and currency trader. McCann would put in £8.5 million and another £2 million for easy-term loans to help supporters buy shares. The fans would be invited to subscribe £5.4 million in total.

The two teams were together. The Celtic Investor Group was formed. There was more money available than ever before but they had still to agree on which strategy to follow. This was the hard part. Low, Moffat, Charles Barnett of PKF and McCann's Glasgow lawyer David Semple met to hammer out a decision. It was a choice between Route One to Goal, the original plan of requisitioning an EGM to get seats on the board and then to issue more shares; or Celtic's Future plc, setting up a parallel company as a vehicle to take over the club; or a combination of the two.

McCann was still keen on Celtic's Future for two reasons: it would assure him of 50 per cent of the club – hardly unreasonable if he was putting up 59 per cent of the total package in investment and loans – and it would involve the supporters from the start. He had taken out newspaper ads and hired a distribution firm to hand out leaflets at matches to assess the desire among fans to invest. The result had been positive. The Route One plan would initially offer shares to existing shareholders and the leading rebel investors, delaying the punters' chance to take part.

Low kept insisting the whole point was to win, to gain power first, otherwise nothing could be done. Celtic's Future could take over the club only after 75 per cent of

Celtic shareholders had voted for a special resolution agreeing to it. Yet here they were struggling to put together 50 per cent to get on to the board. Increasing the number of shares in the club would require a vote of 67 per cent of shareholders, but that was still 1,800 shares fewer than were needed for a direct takeover.

The way to achieve a 67 per cent majority was to have the members of the voting pact disenfranchised, to stop them from voting against it. Although the pact was not in itself illegal it did prevent its members acting freely. By signing the pact they had legally committed themselves never to vote for any resolution which reduced, or diluted, the percentage of shares they owned. This meant that even if the club was in imminent danger of bankruptcy, they were legally bound to vote against a way of saving it if that meant diluting their control. And because they controlled so many shares they could block an attempt by the other share-holders to save the club too.

It would be an injustice to Celtic and its shareholders, so the rebels would ask the courts to stop the pact members from voting against a resolution to increase the number of shares. This would turn the rebels' minority 40 per cent into a majority of 70 per cent and the resolution would be passed.

Eventually the teams agreed to take Route One to Goal. The agreement meant reams of documents, carefully built up for the past two years, could now be released to McCann. Long discussions followed about the exact words to use in any resolutions. Should they go for one share one vote at this stage? Should executive box holders be offered shares in exchange for cancelling their debt? In the end they decided to keep the resolution as simple as possible. They would call for 23 shares to be issued for every two existing shares at a price of £60 a share. The rebel investors would guarantee to buy any shares not bought by other shareholders.

White, the Kellys, Grant and Smith would not be able to afford to pay £60 multiplied by 23 – or £1,380 – for every two shares they owned. In other words, for every share they owned they would have to find £690 if they wanted to keep the same percentage of control they already had. So because of the pact they would be forced to vote against the resolution.

They would have to turn down an immediate injection of £12.5 million into a club already in financial difficulties.

The exact extent of those difficulties was a matter of speculation. The latest accounts were not due out until late September or early October, so the published figures were a year out of date. The rebels' advisers did not know what liabilities the club had under its contract with Superstadia. If the club was in imminent danger of collapse, it would give the courts grounds to stop the pact voting against the proposed share issue.

That year the accounts came out early, on 15 September. The overdraft at 30 June 1993 had been £4,700,000. Already £431,000 had been spent in connection with Cambuslang. After the court action of the previous year, the board had decided to call for the partly-paid shares to be fully paid. Holders of 73 shares – all rebel supporters – had failed to pay so their shares were forfeited.

Four days before the accounts were published Celtic travelled to Kirkcaldy to beat Raith Rovers 1-4. The game was being sponsored by Weisfeld's stepson Michael McDonald, a former schoolmate of Raith's captain, Peter Hetherston. Low and James Dempsey were sitting alongside Willie Haughey, McDonald and Weisfeld. 'I don't know if I want to be photographed with you,' Haughey joked to Low, whom he was meeting for the first time. But there was an element of truth in the joke, even though they drove back to Glasgow together in Weisfeld's chauffeur-driven limo, complete with drinks and TV in the back.

Haughey suggested a further meeting. They met more than a week later in Fazzi's Italian delicatessen and cafe in Glasgow's Cambridge Street. Haughey was a 37-year-old who had worked his way out of the Gorbals to a Mercedes and smart house by building up a refrigeration company. He was street-wise in the world of Glasgow business. He had just bought 44 Celtic shares at £300 a share from a shareholder in Wales and would be attending the AGM.

Haughey wanted to get White and Kelly out and was prepared to invest £1 million. He and Low met a few times more.

McCann arrived from Montreal in September and Low introduced him to a series of shareholders. Nothing could be taken for granted and Fergus had not had much contact with the smaller shareholders. He might have a deal with Dempsey, Keane and the other rebel leaders but it would be a mistake to expect others just to support him blindly. They had to meet him for themselves, get to know him and understand what he was about. Over September and October he met Weisfeld, Betty Devlin, Mrs McLaughlin, Bill Gallacher and others. He had dinner with Hugh Drake and Maureen Blackburn at an Italian restaurant in London's Mayfair. He was at his dapper, charming best but, more importantly, they realised he was a real Celtic man.

Three days before the AGM Celtic went to Perth to play St Johnstone . . . and lost 2-1. A fan, Brian McKenna, slapped Michael Kelly playfully on the back and made an innocent comment. Kelly over-reacted and insisted on the police being called.

Brady decided to resign that night. In another club his record would not have been considered unacceptable but Celtic supporters were ravenous for success, having been starved so long. Brady had thought he knew what he was taking on but he had reckoned without the dire situation Celtic were in. Short of money, torn apart by factions within the club quite apart from those outside, it was impossible to make any real progress.

Next day Kelly hosted one of his regular lunches for a small group of his company's clients and business journalists, including Shennan. It was held in a private dining-room in the replica Victorian hotel, One Devonshire Gardens. He looked drawn and stressed. Brady's departure came up in conversation but the mood was almost one of a bereavement. Kelly's usual jauntiness on these occasions was missing. And at this point he did not know that Joe Jordan had decided to follow his boss and resign. Jordan had been there only three months, brought in by Brady after a major shake-up of the backroom staff.

This time there was no short-list of potential managers made to visit Parkhead for interviews. From the first, former Celtic player Lou Macari was the favourite and David Smith set about negotiating a compensation deal with his current club, Stoke City.

At the AGM shareholders were greeted by noisy fans,

some holding banners. One read: 'Kelly & Co – Time to Go'. Inside, the meeting began with 'something not quite right', to use Kevin Kelly's phrase. He asked Kevin Sweeney, of the law firm of McGrigor Donald, to address the meeting. The board claimed that the signature on one of the proxies was a forgery and that evening it had obtained an interim interdict, or temporary court order, from the Sheriff at Glasgow to prevent it being used.

It was a proxy from James G. Kelly Jr. authorising Matt McGlone, and failing him Fergus McCann, to speak and vote for him. The disputed signature was witnessed by Low and accountant Paul McNeill. The board's lawyer said they had compared it with other signatures by James G. Kelly and consulted a handwriting expert, although an application of interim interdict does not result in a full hearing so the claim was not fully tested in court. The Sheriff had to make an immediate decision without hearing from the other side. But the court order still meant that neither McGlone nor McCann could take any part in the meeting, whether speaking or voting, on behalf of James G. Kelly's shares.

In fact, the proxy *had* been filled out wrongly but it was not a forgery. Because the board had used its veto against the transfer of shares so widely, and the proxies were the only way to represent small shareholders at the meetings, Low had obtained a fistful of proxy forms from every shareholder who agreed. Before the AGM he had filled out a proxy form from James G. Kelly Sr. with the details of James G. Kelly Jr.'s shares. Therefore the signature on the form was the father's and did not match previous signatures from the son.

McCann's legal adviser, David Semple, pointed out that the Canadian knew nothing of what was alleged. But McCann was also the proxy for Mrs Angela McNaught and would therefore be entitled to speak and vote on behalf of her shares.

David Smith was then given a grilling on the accounts. The Bank had now obtained further security over Celtic's assets. As well as being mortgaged it was now subject to what was known as 'a floating charge'. Not only were the Bank entitled to take the ground, they could seize every-thing in it too. Shareholders, including Jimmy Farrell, objected strongly. Smith was questioned on the value put on the ground in the accounts and whether it was really worth £13 million. He was asked how it had been valued and by whom. Consultancy work on Cambuslang had already cost the club £431,000.

Brian Dempsey moved that the directors' fees be cut from £2,500 to £1. He was seconded by Patsy's grandson, Bill Gallacher, and the resolution was passed by a show of hands. But a poll vote overturned it.

Tom Grant and Michael Kelly were due for re-election. In his statement before the vote, Grant tried to explain why he was in the voting pact. Proposed by Jimmy Farrell and seconded by Jack McGinn, he was re-elected on a show of hands by 50 votes to two.

Kelly, proposed by Smith and seconded by cousin Kevin, rejected a call from the floor to withdraw from the voting pact. On a show of hands his re-election was rejected by 35 votes to 26. A poll vote was called for, making his re-election inevitable. To speed up the count, most of those opposed to him did not hand in their voting cards, so he was re-elected by 1,209 votes to ten.

The meeting did not close until 11 p.m., three and a half hours after it began, but by then attention had shifted to the EGM which the rebels had that day requisitioned.

Chapter Twelve

THE FATAL VICTORY – FIRST HALF

I

THE EGM was to be the last major offensive, a final frontal assault throwing all the rebel troops into the battle. Their objective was to be a resolution which, if passed, would dilute the board's control once and for all. For the board to oppose the resolution had serious implications, whether or not all the directors realised it. Directors of such a financially troubled company could not just turn down an immediate cash injection of £12.5 million.

The board had three weeks to set a date for the EGM which then had to be held within four weeks. They took advantage of the full seven-week limit and scheduled the meeting for 26 November. The club had to be recapitalised. The directors knew it, the Bank and the lawyers knew it and had warned them about it. Here was an offer to recapitalise, so how could they refuse it? Their only way out of this jam was to come up with something better. They had to find another white knight, and the only serious candidate for the role of white knight was Gerald Weisfeld. He was now the second largest shareholder with ten per cent. He had a verbal agreement with Brian Dempsey but Low was instructed to tie him in closer to the rebels, so he tried to involve him in the underwriting of the proposed share issue.

Weisfeld was mentioned in a few newspaper stories but was wary of adverse publicity and avoided too high a profile. His support, though, stayed with the rebels.

The club, under its Articles of Association, or constitution, was allowed to have up to 25,000 shares, although so far only 20,000 had been issued. The resolution would authorise the club to have another 225,000 shares, bringing the total to 250,000. The new shares would have to be offered first to existing shareholders, who would have the chance to buy those shares in proportion to the amount they already held. If they decided not to take up their rights or, more probably, if they could not afford to, the shares would then be offered to other shareholders. If they did not buy all the new shares, then the underwriters – McCann, Dempsey and their allies, who would guarantee the success of the share issue – would have the chance to buy.

To guarantee the success of the rights (or share) issue, they had £12.5 million already deposited or guaranteed. Later they would invite supporters to buy shares, bringing the total cash injection into the club to £17.9 million. Nothing like it had ever been proposed or offered to any football club in Britain, let alone Scotland.

The EGM might be a frontal assault but no high command launches an assault without softening up raids first. The rebel plan was for a pre-emptive strike to take out the mass of the opposition before the battle began. They would launch a legal action to bar the five directors in the Shareholders' Trust from voting against the proposals.

The Shareholders' Trust, known by most of the shareholders and fans as the voting pact, forbade its members from approving or voting in favour of any resolution which would decrease the proportions of their shareholding in the club. It meant that a director who decided it was in the best interests of the company to accept an offer of investment could not do so if it involved diluting their percentage, even though his first responsibility was to the company.

Yet the club had £7.2 million of debt which could be called in at any time. Cambuslang, even assuming it ever came about, would not solve any problems until it opened its doors to speculators. In the meantime Parkhead had to be upgraded or another stadium found to rent. The cost of putting Celtic Park in order for *The Taylor Report* could be £24 million. On top of this the ground was mortgaged to the hilt. There was a 'floating charge' over all the club's assets. In effect, everything the club owned was mortgaged. If the club defaulted on its debt, the Bank could seize any property the club had. Then on top of this was a standard security over the fixed assets: the ground, the buildings and the pitch.

Shareholder and descendant of one of Celtic's founders, Dr Hugh Drake, later summed it up colourfully: 'We are still back in the 1880s and the Edwardian Age, whereas Rangers are into the 1990s and facing the 21st century.' He also saw something had gone from the Celtic which his forebear had helped to found and few fans or shareholders had the knowledge of this Sussex lecturer to express it so classically. 'The word "company" comes from the Latin *cum panis* which means "with bread",' he said later, 'and that is how the club started, beginning with tables [meaning the Poor Children's Dinner Table of Brother Walfrid]. But now we have separate tables.'

In the first hearing Betty Devlin and two other shareholders asked the Court of Session to make the pact members reveal the terms of the pact on the grounds that it affected the company they had shares in. The rebels already had copies of the pact, of course, but they were afraid the judge in the second – and main – hearing might stop them using the information in it if they had not obtained it through formal means. The judge decided not to make the order because Mrs Devlin's allies already had accurate information about the pact's contents. That meant the rebels could use the information they already had about the pact document at the main hearing.

Four days later they were in Court 13 of Parliament House in Edinburgh. Advocate Ted Bowen and William Nimmo-Smith QC, representing Mrs Devlin, Hugh Drake and two other shareholders asked the judge, Lord Sutherland, for an interim interdict to prevent the pact members from voting against the resolution at the EGM. The pact was a legally enforceable contract which bound the five directors not to dilute their holdings. Yet if the company was close to bankruptcy, it would mean voting against investment which the company needed if it diluted their holdings in the process. So the shareholders asked the court to stop them voting against. In Dr Drake's words, he thought he 'recognized in the pact a certain abuse of power, an absence of the familial responsibilities which we all share and live by'.

The hearing lasted all day. Low and Farrell were there, but none of the pact members. Donald McFadyen QC, appearing for the pact, suggested three possibilities for Celtic: the club could increase its borrowings, it could increase the equity or shares, or it could share grounds with another club. He twice asked Lord Sutherland to dismiss the action as legally unsound and twice the judge refused. But he also refused to grant the order and refused to insist that the EGM was adjourned. He did not consider that the club was in any immediate danger of bankruptcy.

He did not rule that the pact was legal and at three points in his decision indicated there was a case to be answered. The shareholders' Petition, or request for the order, was not dismissed. They were allowed to continue with the action if they wished, but it would have to be after the EGM.

Farrell later called it a Pyrrhic victory, referring to the battle in ancient Greece when the victors took so many casualties the victory was worthless. 'Really it was a technical victory,' he said, 'and in a sense it was a Pyrrhic victory. Even if the so-called rebels had won it would have been a Pyrrhic victory for them too. Really the whole thing was a defeat for Celtic.'

II

BEFORE the battle itself there would be meetings to see if a full-scale assault could be avoided. They had little hope of success, and neither side stopped preparing for the fight, but they had to be tried. The pace was relentless. The legal action had to be planned, proxies organised. Weisfeld did not want to take centre stage, so proxies had to be arranged for his shares. The more proxies there were, the more chance of having them called to speak at the meeting, and the more chance of winning votes on a show of hands.

Farrell was called to a meeting of the directors who wanted to know what he thought would happen at the EGM and how he would react to it. He was non-committal. In response to what he later described as 'severe cross-examination', he said he reserved his opinion on the court action because he had taken legal advice from an Edinburgh solicitor and two separate advocates.

Kevin Kelly produced a circular. Farrell had time for only a cursory look at it. He could not object to the Chairman sending it out as a circular, but he warned that it would be closely analysed and criticised. Farrell criticised what he felt was a bogus valuation of shares. The circular, put out on the Monday, claimed shares were worth £350, only three years after the board had put a value of £3 on them.

McCann counteracted this with his own circular which included an explanation of the share value by accountants Rutherford Manson Dowds, the same firm which had valued James G. Kelly Jr.'s shares.

Kevin Kelly and McCann met, but the encounter did not go well. McCann was there only to find out when Kelly was going to schedule a meeting. He was impatient for an answer, speaking in short, clipped tones, and his mood was not helped by Michael Kelly being quoted in the media the previous Sunday – two days after the Chairman said they wanted constructive talks – saying confidently they would see off the EGM. Kevin Kelly later complained the Canadian would not even take a cup of tea or coffee, as if he were entertaining a visitor socially rather than having a business meeting.

Grant went to see McCann, trying to find a formula for a peace deal, but Tom was not the problem. Smith, White and Kelly did not appear. Some of Grant's meetings with the rebels were against their express wishes. Low stayed out of the meetings. There was no point. The only person he wanted to see there was Smith, but Smith would not make the first move even though he was the one with the problem. He had to decide whether to accept or reject £12.5 million. He had allowed himself to stumble into Celtic Football Club as deputy Chairman at a time of real crisis and he had since invested around £250,000 in buying shares in a small private company, not even a plc, with archaic Articles of Association.

When a delegation of three directors went to see McCann, Farrell was not included, even though he wanted the whole board to go. The reason was that he was supposed to be 'over-friendly' with Brian Dempsey. He knew Dempsey as a friend and client, and of course briefly as a fellow board member. Farrell felt his omission was insulting but he let it go because he thought the delegation might be a precursor to a full board meeting with the would-be investors.

Jack McGinn was part of the delegation. Like Dempsey, attending with Charles Barnett on the rebel side, he was not afraid to cut across McCann if it became necessary, but the meeting was cordial and constructive. What McCann wanted to know was what the directors needed before they could approve his proposals. The delegation agreed to go back to the board to discuss it and bring the answer to the rebels.

McCann asked for a meeting with all seven directors but they were about to follow the team to Lisbon. The earliest they could get together was four days later, at 11 a.m. on the Friday. This time Farrell was not even informed of the meeting. But then Grant fell ill and was out of action over the weekend, though while at home he managed to dictate a letter of apology for missing the meeting and hoping to arrange another. The rebels waited for the board to appear. When Grant got back to work he found any sense of urgency about a meeting had passed. A month went by without the full board managing to find time to meet the biggest potential investor in the history of the club.

As the week wore on Farrell became increasingly unhappy and told the directors he intended to speak to McCann. He had given his word at the AGM that he would, but he had thought when that promise was made at the AGM the whole board would be meeting McCann not just a delegation. Farrell refused to go to the EGM without talking directly to McCann. The board agreed and on Tuesday McCann went to Farrell's home. They did not discuss the details of the offer, which was well enough known by then, but Farrell asked McCann if he was willing to meet the board.

'Jim,' said McCann, 'my door has always been open. I will meet with you any time.'

Farrell was worried about what would happen in five years when McCann said he would relinquish majority control, but he did not cross-examine the Canadian at that point. The atmosphere was pleasant and courteous. The older man was talking to 'a good Christian gentleman' who had the interests of Celtic at heart. At the EGM he would register his protest at the way McCann had been treated.

A few days before the EGM the directors received a fax from Blantyre Emerald Celtic Supporters Club. It asked: 'Will you as a director and shareholder of Celtic vote in favour of the new capital being offered at the EGM on Friday, 26 November 1993? If your answer to Question 1 was No, why do you not want the money on offer?' Farrell's answer to the first question was Yes because he had no answer for the second question.

On the Friday morning a letter was waiting for him at his office. Headed 'To the Directors of Celtic Football Club', it read:

'It is with great regret that we the travelling Celtic supporters of Ireland must inform you that we can no longer pledge our support to you, the current Trustees of the Celtic Football Club.

Heretofore we had maintained our silence in the hope that you could arrest the decline of our once great club and restore us to our rightful place among the élite of world football. We are in no doubt like us you share a deep love for Celtic. However, neither love or passion will deter the impending catastrophe facing our club. We are a proud and dignified support and do not relish protesting our club but we now feel the pain of progress must supersede the greater pain which will face us if this crisis is not addressed immediately.

This problem can only be tackled by people of strong financial resources, calculated business acumen and creative vision. These qualities, we believe, are not available to the present guardians of Celtic Football Club. The only solution is a swift transfer of control to people of such qualities.

We have no vested interests in who controls the club, the only prerequisite is that the Trustees possess the where-withal, financial or otherwise, to restore Celtic Football Club to its former greatness. We deserve no less. Every Celtic supporter is deeply proud of the club's noble history and traditions. The legacy of family control made the club great. This legacy however has been cruelly exposed by the dramatic changes that have transformed the old order of world football. This is why change is so essential.

Therefore we sincerely request that you step down immediately, act with dignity and honour, pass on your guardianship and join with us as we unite with one common cause, the restoration to glory of Celtic Football Club.'

It was signed 'yours in Celtic' by a long list of Celtic supporters' clubs: Antrim Road in Belfast; the Anton Rogan Club in London; the Ballymena Harp; Ballymena Shamrock; Cookstown Celtic Supporters' Club; Derry No 1; Dungannon; Fruithill, Belfast; Letterkenny, Donegal; Middle Leinster; Monaghan; Dublin; New Lodge; Paul McStay, Cross Guard, Portoferry, Rathburn; Steve Murray, St Peter's, Belfast; St Michael's, Southdown; Tommy Burns, Portadown; Tommy Gemmel, Derry; and Tullyglen, Belfast.

Farrell found the letter 'very poetic'. He did not intend to step down with or without dignity or honour, but wanted to remain as long as he could in order, he said, to try to help restore 'the glory of Celtic Football Club'.

On the day of the EGM, Grant called for the voting pact to be 'binned', saying it had served its purpose. Farrell called it 'a wonderful gesture . . . Tom has been uneasy over the best part of a year . . . he is not happy about Cambuslang and he is not happy with a lot of things. But . . . he is worth every plaudit because it was a most courageous thing . . . Tom is a young married man and really he has got a lot at stake, and I applaud him for speaking his mind.'

Others were less conciliatory than Grant. Kevin Kelly said on radio: 'These rebels, these people are trying to damage the club.' Outside Parkhead a large and noisy group kept up a protest that would last all the way through the EGM. The more extreme jostled and swore at directors as they arrived. The second half was about to be begin.

Chapter Thirteen

THE FATAL VICTORY –
SECOND HALF

A DESCENDANT of one of Celtic's greatest founding fathers fired the first shot in the final set-piece battle of the war. Peter Maley, great-grandson of Willie Maley, one of the club's first players and committee members, was the first to stand up and address the EGM. He held the proxy votes for his father Peter Maley, and had been asked by Betty Devlin to propose the resolution. He began by quoting the minutes of the AGM two years before. Chris White had said then the directors had decided to increase the share capital of the club and had promised a further meeting to bring this about. But, said Maley, it was shareholders who had now been forced to call a meeting.

He outlined the resolution and explained that £12.5 million would be injected into the club and that letters from various banks, including the Bank of Scotland, had been deposited with the club confirming the money was available. 'This figure, as far as I am aware, is the biggest offer of equity ever made to a British soccer club – not just a Scottish soccer club but a British soccer club,' he said.

'I want it to be clear in everybody's mind that the money is not going to be used to pay off existing shareholders or existing directors. The money is going to go straight into this club to be used for various purposes which in my submission this club requires extremely badly.' Applause interrupted him. The Bank had a security over the club's fixed assets 'including the very pitch on which our team plays'. Lou Macari would 'be required to wheel and deal to get new players into this club whereas . . . if this resolution is passed . . . there will be funds available for players.'

There had been Press speculation that shares were worth £400 to £500 but that valuation was based on having the players included in the balance sheet, which they were not. And, said Maley, the only way a figure for players could be realised was to sell them. 'If you do that you are not solving any problems. You are simply throwing the baby out with the bath water.'

Veteran Glasgow lawyer Len Murray seconded the resolution, as the proxy for James G. Kelly Jr. in California. He spelled out the harsh financial facts of life. 'In 1987 Celtic had an overdraft of £15,000. In 1992 the figure was £5 million. To go from £15,000 to £5 million in a period of five years, you might think, took some doing, but it does not stop at that.

'In 1987 the club had no accumulated losses. Indeed, there were accumulated profits of £169,000. The reason for that was the old guard, the last of whom was the late Tom Devlin whose widow is with us, had a different approach because they attempted to balance the books.' But that accumulated profit of £169,000 in 1987 had been turned into accumulated losses of £6 million.

The club had lost more in the one year ending 1992 than in all the previous 103 years of its history put together – £3.2 million. 'To be perfectly fair of course in 1993 the company has done very much better and the loss I think was only £1.3 million.' Nobody laughed.

Comparing the value of Celtic with other clubs brought no comfort for the shareholders. Rangers had a net asset value – that is, the total value of all its assets minus all its liabilities – of £34.8 million. Celtic had a net asset value of £571,000 – a mere one-sixtieth of the club they had once outshone. Even Partick Thistle – 'that incomparable institution of Glasgow' as Murray described it – had a net asset value of £2.2 million – four times the value of Celtic.

In spite of £5.9 million from Celtic Pools in the previous seven years, the biggest source of income after gate receipts, the club – which still had only 20,000 £1 shares – now had liabilities of £7.2 million. 'Personally,' said Murray, 'I have never come across a company that has survived when its liabilities are 360 times its share capital.'

Murray was building up his case with the practised ease of an experienced lawyer. He told shareholders what the club's counsel had told the Court of Session about ground sharing. 'Isn't that a new one for us all – ground sharing? I am not aware, Chairman, this has ever before been suggested to the company in general meetings that in fact they might ground-share, but those were the three possibilities canvassed on behalf of the company yesterday as being possible solutions to this phenomenal illness from which the company presently suffers.'

The next target to come into his sights was Cambuslang. 'There is no sign of the developer having his finance in place.

His summing up was devastating: 'The situation . . . cannot be more grave . . . The position of this company is worse than it has ever been in its life, and it is time . . . that all the cant and hypocrisy came to an end and it is time we faced up to the truth of the situation, because unless there is a massive injection of capital into this company it seems to me that survival is highly unlikely.'

Murray handed the microphone to Fergus McCann. He was there as a proxy for a James Moore of Newcastle-upon-Tyne, not as a man prepared to underwrite the share issue. His lawyer, David Semple, had asked the club to invite McCann to the meeting but no invitation arrived.

He congratulated Mrs Devlin 'for her courage in stepping forward on behalf of Celtic and on behalf of all the shareholders and indeed on behalf of the supporters without whom this club will die'. Then he explained that deposits or bank guarantees already totalled £14.5 million. The share issue would generate the kind of cash needed as a base from which the park could be developed and brought up to the largest capacity seating stadium in Scotland for football, and from which the team could be improved, at the same time that the financial position was put right.

'We are not enemies of Celtic who propose this plan,' he said. 'We are entitled to be as big supporters of Celtic as anyone. The fact that we are not members of two families should not disqualify us from financing and helping to invest in Celtic Football Club.

'I think the threat . . . people may perceive is that this club may no longer be a family business as Dr Michael Kelly referred to it recently in a magazine article. I do not think this club was ever intended as a family business. It was intended as a club for football to improve the situation of poor people in the East End of Glasgow.' These words were greeted with applause.

McCann pointed out that three years before the club had net assets of around £4 million, or £200 per share. Yet the directors blocked share transfers to people they disapproved of and fixed the value of shares at £3. Since then the net asset value per share had slipped to £28.50. The rebels' proposal would underpin the value of shares at £60. Nobody would lose their shares. 'The letter you have seen from the board . . . came from Mr Kevin Kelly several days ago, and he claimed in that letter that the shares were worth £350 – not £3 as in 1990 when things were good but £350 now that things are bad.'

He rounded on the members of the voting pact. 'It is very likely and very unfortunate that the voting pact amongst these five directors which I denounce as being against the interests of the members at large, bad for Celtic's reputation and bad for Celtic's future, will vote against this proposal tonight. In fact, they have agreed among themselves that they will not vote in favour . . . of any increase in capital. I think this is a very regrettable thing. It is obviously designed only to preserve their own position and is not in favour of the club, nor does it reflect truly what director's responsibilities should be.'

McCann agreed that no individual should hold a predominating stake in the club and said he would restrict himself to a stake of 50 per cent. 'If I am paying £8.5 to £10.5 million . . . then I think it is reasonable to have a position of 50 per cent in the club . . . However, I would make sure that all my shares were locked in for a five-year period and not available to anybody else until that five-year period was up.

'And then I would offer them to all the present shareholders and all the new shareholders who may come in . . . so that all the shares would continue to be held by Celtic people. I could not go out and sell to anybody else. Additionally after that time no individual could hold more than ten per cent of the shareholding of the club.' These commitments were already spelled out in letters to the club seven weeks before.

There was a warning for the board and the shareholders. 'I am taking a great risk here by making this proposal for financing,' he said. 'I can say to the board and you people tonight in the hall that this is as good as it is going to get. You are not going to get an opportunity like this again. I do not think I can do more, nor can my colleagues . . . than we are doing. We will not see a dividend for at least three years because of the £6 million carry-over of losses.'

Yet he then made one more offer. 'If you do approve this proposal and decide to buy shares . . . I will personally assist you in doing so up to £2,000 per person towards one-third of the cost of buying those shares. I want to increase your shareholding – you have had it for a long time, why shouldn't you? . . . I also intend if supporters are offered shares to provide "soft" loans to them too. There should be 5,000 or 6,000 or 7,000 shareholders in this club. Why not? They all want to own a piece of Celtic Football Club and why shouldn't they?'

McCann's fellow Canadian Jim Doherty took the floor. He started asking the directors one by one to say why there had been no real negotiations on McCann's proposals as promised at the AGM seven weeks earlier. Kevin Kelly called him to order, saying directors could address the meeting after the shareholders had discussed the resolution.

It was the turn of another descendant of the founding fathers. Dr Hugh Drake's ancestor helped to found the club and his great-uncle saw the first Celtic team play. 'I am Celtic through and through . . . but I do not like the word "rebels". That implies some illegitimate, illegal, dishevelled, dirty, tartan-bedraggled company fighting from without. We are fighting from within . . . we are part of the family tree.'

He was erudite as only a lecturer in English can be. 'It would take the wanderings of a modern Ulysses to find men like Dempsey and McCann and the others,' he declaimed. He was by his own admission an unlikely rebel: 'There I was in Sussex minding my own business in my house overlooking the sea and I got a letter from the board because they were in trouble. Jim and Tom were going to be evicted . . . I had to put down my books and my papers . . . What I found was not a modern corporation squabbling. This was a family squabbling. It was sad, and that is why I got involved.'

Drake fired a series of questions at the directors for them to answer later, including one to Michael Kelly: 'How are you going to make this company up-to-date if it is a family business? Is it an Edwardian corner shop . . .?'

McCann was not going to have it all his own way. Desmond Barr accused him of not telling the whole story. 'I had a meeting with Mr McCann of approximately 65 minutes,' he told the meeting. 'During that particular conversation he gave me his business plan. You have not heard it tonight. You have heard a little bit of it but you have not heard it all . . .

'What he did not say was the fact that he intends to build the stadium which costs £36.5 million. He intends to give so much money to the manager for players. So once we have got rid of the debt and once we have paid the manager money for players we have not got very much money left after that . . . I asked him where he was going to get the money to build the stadium and he said from the bank, that we are going to borrow it from the bank . . . We will be in even more debt if we are going to build a stadium here.

'Then I went on to ask him the question: "Over how long a period are you going to pay this money back?" And he said: "Five years."

'In five years Mr McCann intends to go back to Canada with his money selling his shares, and he also said that he wants £1 million profit . . . I do not see the particular scheme that Mr McCann has is any more credible than the one we have at Cambuslang and as far as I am concerned I am certainly voting against.' This was greeted with applause.

Former player Jim Craig recalled the man who gave his name to the room they were sitting in. 'The club was doing very badly until this genius came along, Jock Stein, and turned the club around.

'Now, he turned the club around with players who were with the club at the time. Unfortunately Lou Macari, in whom I have every confidence and I think will turn out to be an excellent manager of Celtic Football Club, does not have the same quality of players to deal with. He needs players urgently. He is saddled with a team some of whom have been bought at very high prices, some of whom are not up to the task, quite a number of whom are ageing.

'There is a certain element of urgency about this because we have had four very barren years and we can't wait very much longer. If Rangers take the Championship this year that will be six years on the trot they have taken it and I think the fans we can hear outside are getting a bit depressed at the way things are going. But the one thing Lou does need to build a team is money. This scheme certainly provides that money and I would urge everybody to vote for it this evening.' Applause drowned out the noise of the fans.

Kevin Kelly invited the directors to address the meeting. Jack McGinn, as was his habit, began speaking without notes. 'I have spent my time here generally speaking from this part of my body,' he said, pointing to his chest, 'from my heart.'

He was 'a bit of a mongrel in the pack', not claiming the family ties that others did, but he was proud of that and of being the only former employee who had risen to Chairman. He had been disturbed by some of the crowd who had greeted his arrival to Parkhead that night, depressed by the 'horrible tone of language' and the 'disgusting behaviour of some of them'. They did not represent the Celtic supporters he knew.

Two things concerned him about the resolution: he did not believe it was right that people's percentage of ownership should be taken away in one fell swoop, and he feared in case other investors would want their money back at the same time as McCann in five years.

He was not worried for himself because his holding was nominal. 'I have always thought that if the time comes the club do not want me any longer I don't want to be here. If I have served my usefulness and it is time to go I will go happily . . . However, I think it is wrong in my mind that people should come to any company, any house or any kind of business or anything and say: "Because we have got more

159

money than you and you are in a difficult situation give us the keys and we will carry on from here." '

McCann pointed out that he did not intend to take out his money in five years but would leave it in. He would offer his shares to other shareholders at a discount. He told Desmond Barr any bank loans for rebuilding the stadium would be less than the current bank loan of £4.8 million and would be only a small part of financing the reconstruction. In a barbed reference to David Smith's business history and huge debts run up by his previous group, McCann added: 'We are not talking about an Isosceles here.'

It was Jimmy Farrell who answered McGinn's underlying fear: 'You're unhappy as I would be over handing control of this club to someone of the ilk of Robert Maxwell or people of that nature . . . From my knowledge of Fergus McCann, which goes back longer than any of you because I knew his mother and father . . . I think he falls into a quite different category from Robert Maxwell and all the rest of them, these people who are big-money people in England.'

The rebels' offer seemed to Farrell to be 'an unparalleled offer in the history of soccer in Britain and from a man and a group of people whom I know to be Celtic supporters and not lepers, people who were being insulted time and time again'. He again vouched for McCann: 'If he was a Robert Maxwell or somebody like that I would not give him the time of day, but he is a man of dignity . . .'

Farrell outlined the dire financial and legal position, revealing details of the warning they had received from their lawyers as long ago as 1991. 'The company is in serious financial difficulty, and I hope that even at this late moment we can try and solve the situation together. We have all got different interests and different feelings, and have different approaches, but are we not all Celts? Do we not all want somehow or other to get out of this terrible morass? Are we enemies?

'That is the way it looks to me, as if we are, that some people have such a vested interest in controlling the football club that they are blinded to all reason . . . We have not really begun in my view to tackle this problem even yet, and this man has been over here from Canada back and forward like a yo-yo since the summer time.'

Farrell then added his own warning to the two-year-old warning from the lawyers. 'I have a special duty. I am a solicitor and I am supposed to know better. I am supposed to hand out advice to people . . . Over and above that we have got two chartered accountants (Chris White and David Smith) and a professor of economics (Michael Kelly) at this table. So, basically we have, in terms of pending insolvency, a special responsibility. It is a very serious responsibility and we must take it seriously, and we must do something tonight.'

He ended on the subject of the manager: 'Lou Macari is no fool. You can trust Lou Macari with money. He will not throw it around as the previous three managers have done. He will need some money, not the £5 million or £7 million. . . mentioned but he will need some cash.'

Farrell's revelation of the details of McGrigor Donald's advice about increasing the company's capital more than two years before prompted Len Murray to call for an explanation. Chris White said Farrell himself, among others, had opposed an increase because he was anxious about people like Betty Devlin, 'but he seems to have changed his opinion since'.

'But that does not begin to answer my question, with respect,' Len Murray objected. 'It does not begin to deal with it either. I asked a specific question. Was that advice given to the board and, from what Jim Farrell says, are we right then in thinking that the board did nothing to implement that advice?'

Kevin Kelly stepped in: 'I don't think this has anything to do with the meeting tonight.'

'What is the answer, Mr Chairman?' asked Low.

'It is not relevant and that is it,' insisted Kelly. 'What is relevant is what is put forward tonight for voting. That is what is relevant.'

Murray persisted. 'I would respectfully suggest that it is wholly relevant because what is before this meeting tonight is a resolution to increase the share capital and it would appear, from what we have been told, that the board were advised to do that urgently some two years ago. And it would appear also that this is advice that they have ignored . . .'

'With respect,' said Kelly, 'the decision of the board at that time was not to pursue it because things did improve after that date.'

Murray was not going to be put off. He pointed out that the minutes of the AGM on 13 December 1991 recorded that the directors had decided to recommend increasing the authorised share capital and another meeting would be held to do so. 'Is that Minute not right? Which is it, Chairman? Is it what you are suggesting or is it what the Minute says?'

'I am suggesting no decision was made.'

'What does that Minute mean, then?'

'I think this is just prevaricating and misleading the meeting tonight.'

Farrell interrupted to deal with White's point about his concern for Mrs Devlin. He had always been concerned about widows and similar classes of shareholders, and had raised the question of how they would be affected. The Minute was correct and he had never changed his views; the matter had been left in abeyance.

Dominic Keane, the experienced banker, offered another view. 'I believe the directors of Celtic Football Club did not accept the recapitalisation but rather turned to the Bank of Scotland. They brought in David Smith who . . . with his first decision mortgaged the park . . . to ensure that Celtic kept on trading. The following year, as he explained to us at the AGM only a few weeks ago, he offered the Bank the bandit floated charge which would see the company probably through to March or June of next year.

'We now have a situation where players who were bought for fairly expensive transfer fees are now being hived off and I call that asset-stripping, Mr Smith. And I think it is a phrase with which you are familiar. And I accuse the present board first of all of mortgaging the stadium, mortgaging the floating assets of the club and ultimately we are now disposing of – yes, disposing of the players . . . Unless we accept Mr McCann's plan there is no future for Celtic . . .' He asked Desmond Barr what the future was, what the board had told them. 'They have not said anything tonight, Dessy.'

'Could you keep order, please,' protested Kelly. 'You are confusing the whole meeting.'

But Keane started listing the board's offences against the

team. 'That board of directors, there, ladies and gentlemen, authorised payments of £1.6 million for Stuart Slater, sold him for £600,000 to keep the Bank happy and we have now disposed of Andy Payton. Nobody can tell us what we got for him. I suggest it was round about £600,000. We have now taken a 32-year-old valued at £175,000.

'In the days of the late '60s and early '70 Jock Stein disposed of many of his Lisbon Lions in their early twenties. We are now trying to build a team in the 1990s with players of 32 years of age coming from Barnsley. Dessy, please, and others who have yet to change their vote, please change your mind and support us and remove this board of directors and remove them tonight.'

Kelly accused him of changing the mood of the meeting, reminding him of Farrell's words, that they were all Celtic supporters and were trying to come up with a solution.

A heavy man with grey-flecked hair stood up. 'I am Brian Dempsey, friend of Jimmy Farrell.' He apologised to Keane for disagreeing with him but said the evening for him was not about removing the board. 'That is why I have always made my position very clear, that my offer to support Fergus McCann was not to buy myself a seat back on the board . . . I did not see any place for me there, but I genuinely believed rightly or wrongly that unless something was done and done soon there was no way forward.'

He understood better than most the hopes and aspirations of developments like Cambuslang but, as McCann had pointed out, they were tomorrow's solutions and did not answer today's problems. 'I see the issue very simply. There is no doubt the club has an overdraft. I do not think that is a big deal but for the fact that this business turns over less than £9 million and has debts of over £7 million. I do not know how you trade out of that. I wish I did. So I think it needs – and I believe it wants – money urgently.'

Next August somebody would have to decide where Celtic played their football and where the shareholders and fans would watch it. Money had to be invested. Dempsey had been at the meeting with the delegation of three directors and had told them what he now told the shareholders: 'The only thing that is important and has to be a prerequisite of that negotiation was that Fergus McCann would become chief executive. Now, I cannot imagine a situation with anyone putting in the enormous sums of money that he is putting in and he does not have the right to manage his own money.

'I said then to the three members of the board . . . it does not have to be massive wholesale changes . . . There has to be a gradual change-over of people . . . Irrespective of whether I like them or not, irrespective or whether I think they have done a good job or not, they have represented this club for a long number of years and you cannot just discard people like that . . . I am not going to support the wholesale change of directorship but I am here to support one thing, putting money into this business because I believe that it badly needs it.'

He sat down to loud applause. At a point when the meeting threatened to over-heat he retained his usual calm. It had occasionally frustrated journalists looking to get words like 'slammed', 'blasted' and 'lambasted' into the intro of their stories, but on a public platform he always appeared unflappable.

Now it was Tom Grant's turn. His plea to have the directors' voting pact binned had been loudly praised by Jimmy Farrell. Now he would try yet again to be peacemaker. 'I asked [at the end of the AGM] if people would please get together and have meaningful talks. That failed. No matter how often I tried I could not convince others to meet with Fergus McCann.

'I managed to meet with Fergus and I found him to be very helpful. He explained his proposals to me. I had my own doubts about a few of the elements in it. He explained those and I have got to say I am still not entirely satisfied with a good deal of the elements in it. However, there are a good number of elements that would certainly benefit this club. Of that I have got no doubt . . .

'Other directors have told me that they are willing to sit down after this meeting. My frustration is that it may well be too late. I find it very difficult to vote for something that I do not entirely believe in but equally I find it very difficult to defend nothing. I need a better alternative . . .

'It cannot be finished tonight. The arguments must finish tonight but the solutions must start tonight.'

164

Elizabeth Craig asked the Chairman why the board had not met the rebels, accusing them of fear 'of this wee guy over here'. Kelly denied being afraid of McCann. He had met McCann but complained the directors had little chance to talk because the Canadian was in a hurry to protest at earlier remarks by Michael Kelly. 'He did not even have a cup of tea or a cup of coffee or anything.' His answer conjured up an image of the feisty Canadian keen to put his points across while the Chairman was anxious to offer some polite hospitality.

Kelly said they were still open to a meeting and Farrell, who had been excluded from the delegation because of his friendship with Dempsey, suggested having the meeting then, with the seven directors and seven of those interested in investing money. He pressed Kelly to say he was offering a meeting somewhere in that building, even that night. Kelly agreed but said they had to deal with the resolution first.

A familiar figure stood up. 'I am Brian Dempsey, *still* a friend of Jimmy Farrell. I think quite honestly the conduct of this is quite pathetic . . . It is quite appalling . . . to condemn on the one hand because he [Farrell] is a friend and the rest are family. I don't understand the logic of that . . .'

Of the meetings with the board delegation, he said 'I was quick at times if necessary to cut Fergus off, as Jack was too. The fact of the matter was that Fergus wanted to get on and get an answer. He wanted to get a conclusion. Time had passed and we were waiting on a meeting and nothing was taking place . . .'

Dr Michael Kelly brought attention back to the resolution. He was going to vote against because, he said, it robbed shareholders of the value of their shares. Shares had recently changed hands at £350 a share.

'And did these people get their shares transferred?' interrupted Betty Devlin.

'We are discussing now, Betty, the value of the shares . . . Share transfers or share sales have taken place at a value of up to £350 a share. Now, if these resolutions are carried, when the shares are issued the shares will be valued at £60 a share. So at that time with 250,000 shares floating around it will be extremely difficult for anyone to sell any of their shares at even £60 a share.'

In order to be fair, he said, McCann should make an offer for all the shares in the company. He accused McCann of wanting control without paying an entry price. Then he accused Keane of letting 'the mask slip. . . That was the hostility and that was the aggression that was portrayed at the last meeting here.'

'That is the frustration, Dr Kelly, of a Celtic supporter,' replied Keane.

'No, it is much more than that. It is a personal aggression and hostility that has been portrayed against the board and individuals in the board . . .'

'There is hostility within the board, Michael, from member to member,' said Mrs Craig to applause.

As Kelly was replying a young man jumped up. 'My name is Willie Haughey . . . and I want to say that there are people here who will underwrite right now any director who would like to sell his Celtic shares for £350 a share, and I will be part of that.' Low was sitting between Haughey and Weisfeld with his stepson. Haughey was inadvertently giving the board ammunition when the rebels' calculations had shown the shares had little in net assets behind them.

'That is an incredibly generous offer, and let me be the first to reject it,' said Kelly. 'I don't want to sell my shares in Celtic. My shares are far more important to me than money . . . but as a director I could not recommend shareholders to accept Fergus McCann's offer when an offer like yours is on the table. . . I don't think there will be a shareholder in the room who would want to vote for the resolution because your intervention completely undermines any logical reason for accepting it.'

'The offer is only available to directors,' said Haughey.

'There again that is something that no director could accept because that is unfair to the vast bulk of share-holders . . .'

'The minute you signed the pact, that was unfair to shareholders.'

'Lord Sutherland does not agree with you.'

'Lord Sutherland is not a Celtic supporter or a share-holder.'

'That is why he can judge the case objectively . . . the Court of Session yesterday threw out every single aspect of the petition . . . So the pact is absolutely and utterly legal . . .' He asked McCann: 'How can you come along here the next day and appear to be totally reasonable and fair and want to deal with us when in fact you wanted this decision tonight to be taken with 40 per cent of the shareholders deprived of their votes?'

'Do you want me to answer the question?' asked McCann.

'No, it was a rhetorical question. I want the other shareholders to evaluate that argument . . .' He then attacked the way the campaign had been run: 'There has been a persistent attempt over the last two years which continues tonight to damage the club financially. The overdraft is consistently exaggerated, the debts are exaggerated . . . Look how the fans have been wound up in this . . .

'Fergus, you appear to think that your activities and the demonstrations are unrelated. I simply cannot accept that when I see professionally produced banners, professionally produced posters and what appears to me to be clearly organised activity. I am not saying, Fergus, that . . . you are spending money on these demonstrators and I am not saying that you are organising them but . . .'

Matt McGlone owned up: 'Mr Chairman, I have been doing these things along with other certain Celtic supporters who have organised the "Celts For Change Group" because we do not think you are healthy for the club and we do not believe in you . . . I will categorically tell you that nobody else in this room was involved in it.'

Kelly attacked McCann's plans: 'I do not like the idea that you want to be chief executive for five years. I do not like the idea that you want 50 per cent plus control of the club. I think that one of those is bad enough but the two combined in one person is extremely dangerous. I have not seen enough of your business plan or your capital structure to be able to discuss it, but from what I have gleaned I have doubts about that as well . . .' Yet details of the proposal had been sent to the board's financial advisors the previous summer.

Chris White, speaking for the first time at the meeting, dismissed the claim in Betty Devlin's petition that £25 million was needed to make Parkhead meet the requirements of *The Taylor Report.* 'Possibly, possibly, £2 million needs to be spent in order to comply with Taylor, possibly

'... I think the club is stable thanks to the direction which the present directors are giving the club . . . You shake your head, Betty, but I think maybe you are being misled in your thinking.'

Betty Devlin was 70-plus years young and nobody was going to tell her she was being misled. 'No . . . Christopher. I make up my mind on things and nobody tells me what to do. This is from my heart. I am an out-and-out Celtic supporter.'

'Yes, as I am too, Betty.'

'As your father and your grandfather, as my husband and my father-in-law, although nobody remembers them. But this is from my heart, and I just feel that you are not going about your business in the right way and the club is not benefiting.'

Tom Grant put a question to his fellow pact members: 'If Michael was willing to accept the offer that was put on the table tonight would the Shareholders' Trust release him to accept it?'

'That is a deeply hypothetical question because I certainly have rejected the offer . . .' said Kelly. 'As you know you are not going to sell your shares and I am not going to sell mine.'

A little later Matt McGlone asked Grant if he would consider selling his shares to perhaps Willie Haughey or somebody else if he could be released from the pact.

'Yes, if the pact would release me I would certainly have to consider that offer.'

'Would you like to be out of the pact just now, Tom?'

'I have said so earlier, Matt. I think it has served its purpose. I think it should be binned.'

'And it is certainly immoral?'

'I wouldn't say that. I would say it has served its purpose.'

'Is it unethical?'

'No, I would not have entered into it in the first place if I had thought that.'

'But if you could sell your shares would you consider it?'

'I would certainly consider it, yes.'

Low asked to hear from the deputy Chairman. Smith's reply rambled: 'At the end of the day the proposal that helps the club will be the one that succeeds and gets the support of shareholders. It is as simple as that. It doesn't matter what we say huffing and puffing about it just now . . . The position of the club is not as dire as it is represented. That does not in any way mean the health of the club could not be better. Of course it could . . .

'Would more money help? Yes, of course it would. It would be silly to say otherwise, but at the end of the day the money that comes into the club, if indeed any money comes in, has got to be acceptable to the people who are the club, whether they be shareholders, board members or anything else . . . I will vote against the resolution not because I do not think that we could not make progress if more money was available to the club – of course I think that – but as it happens I do not think the club needs nearly as much as the figures quoted.

'I think much more significant progress could be made in terms of how the club's affairs are run with much smaller sums of money made available to the club. So I think the figures which are being quoted and quantities and amounts of money are almost unnecessary . . . I'm never quite sure if it does much good to have too much money . . . That is certainly not what the club needs right now . . .'

Low did not mince words: 'What we have just had there is five minutes of misleading, arrogant twaddle, absolute rubbish. Your counsel yesterday in the Court of Session described these resolutions as a rescue package. He said that your means of dealing with Celtic's financial problems was to borrow more money or issue more shares or to sell more players. Your means of dealing with Taylor was to refurbish Parkhead or to ground-share – no mention of any of this Cambuslang rubbish.

'You as deputy Chairman of this company have had seven weeks to speak to Mr McCann and you have done nothing. You do not return calls. As a professional person you have not approached him, you've said nothing and done nothing. You have made yourself unavailable. Why have you not met Mr McCann? Why have you not discussed these resolutions with him? Why have you not sought to deal with the problems that you say you are having with these resolutions? Why wait until after the event?'

No answer was forthcoming. Instead the Chairman proposed going to the vote. McCann stood up to thank Kelly for his conduct of the meeting and even apologised if he had talked too long. But he supported Low's questions to Smith: 'Where were you? You were the Vice-Chairman and you had a responsibility . . . This is the only offer which will be made. All discussions with the board have come to nothing. Attempts I have made over five years have come to nothing. You are the only people who can decide on this. You are the shareholders and so I ask you to make the decision tonight.'

Resolution 1 was put to a show of hands. The result was even at 47 each, but as the resolution needed a two-thirds majority it was lost. A poll vote would produce a similar result. The board had won yet again, so they thought. So the rebels thought. In fact, the board had won the vote but lost the war. Their final victory was fatal to them.

Chapter Fourteen

CHANGE FOR CELTS

I

THE board had been pelted by the fans as they left the EGM, but the rebel shareholders were as depressed as they were angry. Low had been convinced before the EGM that the board were close to being beaten and would come under so much pressure because of the financial situation that they would come to the rebels for a deal. He was wrong, but not completely. After the final surrender Grant asked why Smith had not gone to the rebels to talk. Had he done so, events might have concluded more easily for the pact members. Smith may be believed that to do so was a sign of weakness. Low had the same attitude. Outside of shareholders' meetings, he did not speak a word to Smith until it was all over. The difference was that Smith *was* in a position of weakness and should have acted.

It took Low most of the weekend that followed to realise the board were in fact finished. They had been offered £13.8 million to put into the club and had turned it down. If they had a better alternative they would have brought it out by then. They had to come up with something to justify to the Bank why they rejected a massive cash injection. Although the board had appeared to win the November EGM, that was in reality when they finally lost.

The rebels were at the gates. Dempsey and McCann had announced their withdrawal but had simply pulled back out of sight awaiting the moment they knew would come. Inside the citadel the beleaguered defenders' supplies of time, money and options were running out. Outside the citadel was now a besieging army of fans. Week after week their discontent was visible and vociferous. To them, the board emerged from the EGM exposed as being more interested in self-preservation than in Celtic Football Club.

Even before that meeting the discontent had begun to take on a more organised form. Those who had accused the rebels of stirring up the fans who chanted outside Parkhead during shareholders meetings, or abused directors when they arrived for matches, misunderstood the mood on the terraces and even in the stands. The supporters produced their own leaders. All they received from the rebel faction was moral support – they needed nothing else. 'There was no organisation,' said one of the founding Celts For Change, Brendan Sweeney. 'We had to organise it ourselves.'

On 19 October, between the AGM and EGM, a group met in McConnell's Bar. They were Matt McGlone of *Once A Tim*, Gerry Dunbar of *Not The View*, Brendan Sweeney, David Cunningham and John Thompson. They were already very active supporters: two were fanzine editors, Cunningham was already a representative of a supporters' club, and Sweeney had been handing out leaflets in Perth at the match against St Johnstone, which proved to be Liam Brady's last. With them were Bill Gallacher, now on the committee of the Celtic Shareholders Association, and Paul McNeill, David Watt and Low as observers.

'We wanted to form an action group to put pressure on the board,' said Matt McGlone, a screen printer with the voice and looks which would make him a natural spokesman on television. They had found a rapidly growing anger among the fans. They came together to discuss ways of turning that anger into properly directed pressure.

With their own money they took a small newspaper advertisement and booked one of the smaller rooms in the City Halls at Candleriggs, expecting about 30 people. Fifty turned up. For their next meeting they booked a room that would hold 50. Four hundred people turned up. The janitor hurriedly opened up a larger room for them. Other than Thompson, who was an account executive, none of them had any experience of public speaking. Sweeney was a railway clerk, Cunningham was an electronics engineer and Colin Duncan, who joined them a few weeks later, was a fabricator. They were like Bill Gallacher, the kind of West of Scotland working men it is all too easy to underestimate.

There had been other pressure groups formed, including a coalition of them under the name Celts For Change. Nearly two years earlier, in the run-up to the EGM which attempted to remove Grant and Farrell, Gerry Dunbar of *Once A Tim* and Willie Wilson of Save Our Celts, had met at Low's home to discuss what might be done. At various times the different groups occupied the limelight but they had not yet fully commanded a mass support. Now the time was ripe for a major campaign. Celts For Change mushroomed immediately. McGlone, Cunningham, Thompson and the others had tapped into a reservoir of frustration that swept them along. Celts for Change was self-funding, with pails passed around at meetings. The money came in, literally, in buckets.

Demonstrations were staged at the main entrance to Parkhead before home matches, and up to 2,000 fans joined them. During the EGM they organised their own Walfrid Soup Kitchen and kept a noisy vigil outside Parkhead from 6 p.m. till after 11 p.m. Protesters were given a voucher for a free soup and a pie.

A 24-foot banner was made, which read 'Back the Team, Sack the Board' which they planned to take into the ground for the St Johnstone game on 18 December and hold up across the Rangers end. There were usually 2,000 spectators there but they had asked for it to be kept clear and there were only 200 that day. They and their banner were stopped, but the attendant publicity rebounded on the board.

'Sack the Board' became a slogan, a chant and an anthem. It became so well known that seven days after Fergus McCann took over a Parkhead, the slogan reached national politics. Labour leader John Smith told the Scottish Labour Party conference the electorate's message for John Major's government was 'Sack the Board'.

Confident of support, Celts For Change booked Govan Town Hall and 1,200 fans crowded into the meeting. It was time to step outside the confines of their meetings and protests at the ground. Next day 500 of them protested outside the Bank of Scotland's main office in Glasgow with placards saying 'Fergus McCann – our £13m friend for life' in parody of the Bank's advertising campaign.

Ireland, north and south, was a vital part of Celtic's support. Every Saturday, and even midweek, coach-loads of fans would board the ferry at Larne to sail to Stranraer and drive up the winding roads of Scotland's south-west coast to Parkhead or the other Premier League venues. Celts For Change contacted supporters' clubs in the north of Ireland and were invited to address a meeting there. But they were understandably nervous about the security implications of holding a large Celtic meeting in Belfast. The Irish supporters then suggested a meeting on the ferry itself.

In the early hours of New Year's day, having sacrificed some of the pleasures of over-indulging on Hogmanay, the Celts For Change committee were breaking the speed limit on the almost deserted road to Stranraer. They were catching the early ferry which would be returning with hundreds of Celtic fans flooding over for the traditional Old Firm match. On the return trip they addressed a noisy meeting of 1,100 fans.

The majority of the Irish fans had not seen the kind of stories which were by then commonplace in the Scottish Press and on television. Most of their information had come from *Celtic View*, which had been used by the club the way the Kremlin had used *Pravda*. They had been fed a 'diet of deception', in McGlone's words. They began the meeting by asking questions and ended it by shouting suggestions for what to do to the board. The suggestions did not involve conventional business – or even medical – procedures.

Early that month they held their largest meeting yet. Sixteen hundred people filed into the largest room in the City Halls. Ever since the Govan meeting people had been talking about a boycott. Many fans were already staying away from the games but McGlone, Cunningham, Colin Duncan and the others did not believe at that point a boycott was feasible. Even if all 1,600 stayed away from the games it would be only a dent, not decisive, and then it would be difficult maintaining the momentum. 'We wanted to keep a boycott as a last resort,' said Sweeney.

Celts For Charge wanted to work with the official supporters organisations. A meeting was arranged with representatives of the Affiliation of Registered Supporters Clubs at the Watermill Hotel in Paisley to see if there was any common ground. They concluded that they shared the same views and agreed to keep talking.

They met again on 16 January along with the Celtic Supporters' Association. Cunningham was asked to leave because he was an ordinary member of the Association. The others protested but he agreed to leave because it was more important that the meeting went ahead. The meeting produced a joint Press statement and a week later they met in the Kelvin Suite of the Grosvenor Hotel. To their surprise, Celts For Change were accused of undermining the authority of the official organisations. When Jim Brodie and Peter Rafferty, leaders of the official supporters' organisations, left to be greeted by the media outside, they came close to implying that Celts For Change was working for Dempsey and McCann. 'That was when we decided to go over their heads,' said Duncan. 'We had been approached by people in the Affiliation and Association who felt their views were not represented.'

They began a series of small meetings with groups of Celtic supporters all over Scotland, winning enthusiastic backing each time. They even set up a post office box number and were receiving 200 letters a week. Within eight weeks they had around 8,000 supporters, including the Irish fans, more than half the size of the membership of the official organisations. On 4 February they travelled to Dundalk to meet representatives of 52 supporters clubs; 51 of them decided to back Celts For Change. 'That's when we knew we had won,' said Cunningham. 'We had won over the hardest people to convince. They were tremendous people who had just been misinformed.'

'We were on a high,' added Duncan. Unfortunately their phone bills nearly quadrupled in cost, and wives, families and even employers had their tolerance tried to the limit. The pace was relentless and the meetings were only a fraction of the work. They had to stuff leaflets into envelopes for mail-shots and run to the post to ensure they arrived before Saturday's game.

Ireland, which had added the word 'boycott' to the English language, provided the backing necessary for a successful boycott of Celtic. 'Once Ireland was behind us we knew we had won,' said Duncan. 'From there on we were heading for the boycott.'

The official organisations had suggested a letter writing campaign and a walk-out from matches after 60 minutes as a protest. The Celts had tried letters early on and objected to walk-out on two grounds: first, it would not deprive the board they were trying to unseat of money and, second, there was a potential safety hazard. Fans would have to leave past fellow supporters who might object to the walk-out. They did not want to risk arguments or even scuffles and fights breaking out.

A boycott was now unavoidable. A continuing boycott had been applied to *Celtic View*. From a print run of 20,000 a week, sales had plummeted to 8,000. The question was: When, and how well would a boycott of games work? Nearly 20,000 Celtic supporters still paid their hard-earned money week after week, in spite of having their patience for results on and off the field sorely tested. If they had not drifted away by now, could they be persuaded to stay deliberately? It was one thing to shout support in a meeting or to demonstrate before going into a match, but the whole point of being a Celtic fan was to watch the Bhoys play.

Rumours were starting to circulate that Haughey and Weisfeld were ready to make a bid. McGlone and Duncan met the two businessmen and Michael McDonald. They were prepared to put up £3.6 million to buy out the board and their supporters. 'We asked them to give us seven days and we would save them three and a half million pounds,' said Duncan.

Weisfeld was not so sure. He felt the board would have to receive something before relinquishing control.

II

ALMOST immediately after the EGM the board began discussions with Willie Haughey. The information came to Low directly from Haughey who had a series of meetings with him over the same period. Haughey wanted to buy the board out and was prepared to put up £1 million. He was having meetings with Smith. Could Low get Dempsey and McCann involved? The answer was a definite no. Haughey approached Dempsey direct and the answer was still the same.

On 14 February came the message that Kevin Kelly and Tom Grant wanted to talk to Dempsey and McCann. They did not want to sell to Haughey and Weisfeld but they were coming under greater and greater pressure to do so and the club was fast approaching the brink of receivership. With Dempsey in Los Angeles, Kelly and Grant met Dominic Keane and Low.

The race began to re-assemble their package before Smith could reach a deal with Haughey and Weisfeld. Low briefed Kelly and Grant carefully about what to do. They were to use the pact which had been used for so long to block the rebels to foil any attempt by its other members to sell out. Instead Kelly and Grant, financed by the rebels, would offer to buy up to half of the shares of the others. In a stroke that would block Weisfeld, deny the directors an undeserved profit and give Dempsey and McCann control.

Smith tried to get Kelly and Grant to the Edinburgh offices of corporate lawyers, Dickson Minto, for a 'discussion'. In fact, Haughey and Weisfeld were waiting there to conclude a deal. Kelly and Grant were told to refuse the invitation. Dempsey, calling from Los Angeles, and McCann from Scottsdale, Arizona, pressed for any deal to be blocked while they reassembled the funds rejected by the directors less than three months earlier.

The pressure on Kelly and Grant was increased. They were told they would be asked for personal guarantees, putting their homes and savings at risk. They were told the Bank of Scotland were about to bounce Celtic cheques. But they refused to sell and then made their offer to buy shares from those who did want to sell.

In the last week before the collapse of the old guard, Smith held his ill-advised Press conference to announce the 'funding' for Cambuslang to the media, before informing the whole board and without informing Haughey. Within days the 'funding' package was exposed as worthless. The Bank of Scotland set a deadline for the directors to sign personal guarantees and to pledge their shares as security for the club's debt. The Celts For Change boycott was applied for the first time, with a dramatic impact. If Rowland Mitchell at the Bank had any doubts about the action he was taking, the attendance figures should have dispelled them.

Weisfeld flew into Scotland from Australia and agreed a £3 million personal guarantee against the overdraft, but it was over-ruled an hour later by a majority of the board: Kelly, Grant, Farrell and McGinn. They then held an emergency board meeting to strip White and Smith of all executive responsibilities immediately and to accept £1 million from the McCann team. Hurried phone calls and faxes arranged for the equivalent number of dollars to be wired from New York. It arrived at the bank next morning and the last signature was put on the paperwork with eight minutes to spare.

But the story was still not over . . .

III

WHILE McCann and Low were working to beat the Bank's High Noon deadline, the defenders were still defiant. Smith arrived at Glasgow airport ready to fight. But they were not long at Parkhead before they realised they were beaten men. Their attention turned to how much they would receive for their shares. More determined men would have fought on. They might have challenged the legality of the previous day's board meeting, called at such short notice. But they didn't. Instead the haggling began.

Dominic Keane was handling the negotiations at Parkhead. McCann and Low were the hawks in the rebel alliance and were for giving the directors nothing at all. But Low accepted the argument of the others that they had to pay an 'entry price'. He gave Keane authority to go up to £1.4 million for all their shares. The three defeated pact directors were put in separate rooms to weaken their bargaining power.

Smith was still the main concern. He had to be removed from the equation. The rebels were still worried about Weisfeld. Would he come back for a fourth attempt? He was

178

still Celtic's largest individual shareholder with ten per cent of the club, bought from Dempsey less than a year earlier. He had supported the McCann-Dempsey alliance in November but since then he had launched his own forays against the target.

To Low's surprise, Smith would not deal on his own. Either from principle or because of the complications it would cause, he refused to sell out the other two. But White and Michael Kelly could still have done a deal with Weisfeld. Michael Kelly had not yet been stripped of any executive powers because he had played his cards very close to his chest. It was not clear how involved he was in the actions of Smith and White.

They wanted what had been the price paid at the height of the campaign, or £300 a share, for themselves and their families, which would have cost the rebels around £2.5 million. The private response of the rebels was not a business term but it would have been clearly understood on the terraces. Instead the directors were offered a total sum, less than £2 million, which they could divide between themselves and their families in whatever proportions they agreed between themselves.

It meant the rebels acquired a majority stake for what, compared to the price the year before, was a bargain. But when measured against the net assets Celtic had left, it was generous. But the less immediate members of the families could not be bound by the deal, and there was another buyer in the market. Weisfeld already had about ten per cent of the club but he was still buying shares. Some members of the families sold to him at £275 a share. Within weeks his stake was up to 18 per cent and in a little over a month it was 23.5 per cent.

Their willingness to sell to Weisfeld was a sign that Dominic had negotiated a tough deal. But it was not tough enough for Fergus McCann. To him it was tantamount to rewarding the directors for what they had done to the club. When he reached Parkhead about 2 p.m., his verdict on what the directors should receive was simple. 'Not one thin dime,' he said.

In the players' reception room on the ground floor Kevin Kelly and Jack McGinn had been waiting since the board meeting had split up into the negotiations. They thought McCann was coming to Parkhead to sign the deal. Instead Low walked in and announced: 'They're getting nothing.'

'Oh, no,' said Kelly, putting his face in his hands.

Outside Dempsey pulled Low aside. Both knew that by objective standards it was a great deal, but in football – on and off the field – few can remain objective. And this was about more than football. This was about Celtic: a club which from its very beginnings had been asked to express the feelings and aspirations of whole communities. First, the community of Irish Catholics in the West of Scotland. As the club grew it carried the hopes of supporters throughout Scotland and England and in the soccer-starved lands of Ireland, Canada and America.

Too much time, money, effort and most of all emotion, had been expended in the long, rocky progress to Paradise for the outcome to be determined by just another business deal. This was not business. This was personal.

The two men held a hurried meeting. Dempsey reminded Low that Smith, Kelly and White could still go to Weisfeld if there was no deal sewn up. 'Speak to him, David.'

Low did some sums. He calculated that in total support they could now command 87 per cent of the club if all of White's and Kelly's supporters accepted the offer. He put his figures to McCann. Barnett of Pannell Kerr Forster supported the argument. So did Keane, now visibly anxious. The Scots-Canadian was nothing if not decisive. 'OK,' he said. 'Go for it!'

It was time for the lawyers to come in. At no point did McCann or Low meet their opponents. They did not want to speak to them. Outside what had begun as a slow trickle of fans that morning had grown to a flood. They were no longer there to boo and jeer a board they blamed for failure, they were there to cheer and toast Dempsey and 'McCann the Man'. Some lifted bottles, in at least one case champagne, or cans in salute towards the brick frontage with the green letters that spelled out the name of the club they felt was theirs once again. McGlone summed up the general view: 'It was one of the greatest moments of my life.'

At about 7 p.m. the former rebels, now in control, and the remaining directors went up to the restaurant inside Parkhead named after Brother Walfrid who had worked so hard to keep his Poor Children's Dinner Table going. At this dinner table they sat down to prawn cocktail followed by fish and chips rounded off with champagne and cigars. Around the table were McCann, Dempsey, Low, John and Dominic Keane, his business partner Jack Flanagan, Barnett, and three of the surviving directors Kevin Kelly, Tom Grant and Jimmy Farrell.

A few tables away were the defeated side: David Smith and Michael Kelly with the lawyers from Dickson Minto. White had lost his appetite.

Low always focused on someone in the opposition. In the battle for Bremner it had been former Chairman James Rowland Jones. In the battle for Celtic it had been David Smith. But he never approached or spoke to him until it was over. To him, making the first approach is a sign of weakness. Seeing Smith in the restaurant he made a point of walking past his table. As he did so, he winked at Smith.

When the cigars were passed around, Low, now with his jacket off to reveal blue braces and St Aloysius' tie, took his Havana across to Smith's table and asked him for a light. 'I'm sorry I don't smoke,' said Smith.

McCann did not waste that much time on the man all evening. His only words to him were: 'Goodbye, Mr Smith.' By comparison he was positively talkative to Kelly: 'We're all glad you're going, Michael. You've been a disaster for Celtic.'

It was approaching midnight and still the fans waited outside, spirits not dampened by the steady rain. It was McCann, so often thought of as terse and clipped of speech, who summed up the day, but he felt he could not say it to the crowd outside. An ebullient Dempsey, totally relaxed with the fans, offered himself: 'I'll say it then.' And going out to the long-suffering supporters, he announced: 'The game is over. The rebels have won.'

Chapter Fifteen

REBELS INSIDE THE GATES

I

THE supporters cheered and clapped and celebrated. The boycott was lifted. The fans were now impatient only for a home game in which to show their appreciation. The battle really was over. The rebels really had won. But the work had only just begun. They had gained control of the boardroom. Now they had to bring the company under control.

An immediate difference between the old régime and the new showed itself. Where the old régime had clung tenaciously to their seats on the board, the new régime made no rush to become directors. This was not modesty or false humility, but a realistic appraisal of the situation. Fergus McCann was to be managing director and as the largest investor had to be on the board. Dominic Keane was a former banker and the club's relationship with its bank was one of the most pressing concerns. Low had no romantic ideas about a seat on the Celtic board. He knew directorships were responsible positions, duties as well as rights. There was a great deal of sorting out to do within the company itself. That could best be done in the back room.

Brian Dempsey had always said his main intention was not to get back on the board. Once he had been kicked off it, it was reasonable that he would be unable to work with the previous board. There is no doubt, though, he would have loved to be on the board once it changed, but there were a number of reasons for his deciding against. First, he was a businessman and like Low he realised a period of upheaval was just beginning. Second, there was his health and his family. It is unusual that he has been able to build and run a successful group of companies while admitting that he is a worrier. Most businessmen learn to switch off worry at a certain point; it is the only way to survive the stresses. In Brian's case, the stresses were beginning to take their toll.

In addition, he is a genuine family man and the campaign for Celtic had added to an already hard-working régime that meant long days away from his wife and children. He was determined to put that right.

Third, though, was his relationship with Fergus. Both men are leaders not subordinates. They had both built up their businesses from nothing. Their styles are quite different. Brian is sociable, voluble, enjoys conversation and the company of those who also appreciate it, such as journalists. Fergus is quiet, terse, brusque on occasion, and feels less need to win people over. Celtic suddenly had two potential leaders at the same time when it really needed one for the immediate future.

McCann inherited a legacy of debt, mismanagement and misinformation. Almost immediately after 'Takeover Day' – or Good Friday as many fans called it – a team of accountants from Pannell Kerr Forster, a firm airily dismissed by David Smith at the last AGM, as 'relatively small' in spite of being the seventh largest accountancy firm in Britain, moved into Parkhead. They were allowed to enter offices and open filing cabinets. They pored over files, examining letters, contracts, invoices and bank statements. Their task was to study every document that would enable them to present McCann with an accurate and up-to-date picture of Celtic's true financial situation.

Nothing was overlooked, from the profit and loss figures to the cost of Cambuslang consultancy fees, from the players' salaries and pensions to the number of company cars, from sponsorship deals to match-day advertising, everything had to be read, added up, checked and listed. Nothing was too small, such as the cost of an executive restaurant table, or too controversial, such as the best estimate of the outcome in the Terry Cassidy case. Within weeks, a report nearly two inches thick thumped on to the managing director's desk.

The position was worse than the published figures had suggested. The club had made another six-figure loss since the last accounts appeared and it owed nearly £8 million, more than £5 million of it to the Bank, costing the club around £30,000 a month in interest charges alone. Yet the internal management accounts had put the club down as making a six-figure profit in the same period. The financial investigators estimated Celtic's net assets at less than a third of the figure in the management accounts.

Celtic was well over its overdraft limit. Just before the takeover the limit would have been £5 million but for an additional clause in the agreement with the Bank. For every transfer deal in which the club received more than £250,000, the overdraft limit would be reduced by half the total amount. So Stuart Slater's transfer in September 1993 for £750,000 and Gerry Creaney's in January 1994 meant that instead of £5 million, the overdraft limit was less than £4.4 million.

Most of the difference between the two pictures of Celtic's situation was due to how the Cambuslang fees and players' signing-on fees were treated by the different accountants. Fees to the various consultants involved in the Cambuslang stadium project had already cost more than £430,000 but they had been around three-quarters of the Celtic's net assets by then – but they had been included in the previous accounts as a recoverable current asset – in effect, money they could get back instead of money spent and gone. And the internal management accounts spread the cost of signing-on fees across the whole year even though they were actually paid in a lump sum.

Three-quarters of the payroll cost went to players and football management staff. Players accounted for more than £2 million, including signing-on fees, with wide variations. The salary difference between top and bottom was more than 750 per cent. Lou Macari was reported to believe the wage structure was 'very high'.

The club had over-estimated its income, expecting £100,000 more for income from radio and television rights than they received. But it also became clear that the club had been selling itself short. Terry Cassidy had once expressed a similar view to Shennan in a newspaper interview: 'I don't think you should be panicked into a low value for any product,' he said. Yet some of the sponsorship and advertising deals gave Celtic a poor return and others had no built-in mechanism for monitoring the returns to the club. The club's commercial side was still underperforming. The retail shops at Parkhead and at Dundas Street were doing only a quarter of the business that Rangers shops did. In the previous year two members of staff had been dismissed after stock discrepancies were found. Even allowing for the boycott, the returns from catering and from *Celtic View*, which had been transferred to a contract publishing firm in 1993, were poor.

Only £1.5 million had come in from the sale of 7,000 season tickets, costing between £170 and £270, for the current season. Celtic had been slow to understand the value of season tickets to their cash flow. They had been reluctant to push them hard because they felt most supporters could not afford one. Celtic are now pursuing a deal with a credit company which would allow easy terms for fans buying season tickets while giving the club the advantage of receiving a lump sum before the season starts. By the beginning of 1994 the number of executive club members was down to 280, less than three-quarters of capacity.

Only days after the accountants' arrival, one newspaper splashed a story headlined 'Tax Probe at Celtic', but the only investigation had been part of a long-standing nationwide inquiry. The Inland Revenue's Special Office had a team of inspectors looking for any tax-dodging in British football, such as under-the-counter payments to players, or interest-free loans later written off, or payments to service companies or agents on behalf of players. The Inland Revenue had approached Celtic six years earlier and the board had quite properly asked accountants Ernst & Young to investigate. Their report concluded that there was only one possible infraction of the rules for the whole of the five years up to 1992 and the club's accounts had allowed a little over £50,000 for any under-payment of tax.

Some paperwork could not be found, including details of David Smith's agreement to pay Stoke City compensation for the loss of Lou Macari and his backroom staff, and vouchers from the Football Trust dating back to the Mid-Eighties which meant Celtic had failed to claim back corporation tax it was owed.

One item, especially, surprising the grey-suited accountants, Celtic held 5,000 shares in its historic rivals, Rangers Football Club.

The most immediate decision for McCann to take concerned the stadium. For nearly two years the Bank had expressed concern about how a new stadium would be funded, but the 'field of dreams' had been pursued. Half a million pounds had already been spent on it. Should he carry on with it? The answer was a firm 'No'.

But it still left Celtic with only five months to comply with *The Taylor Report* and make the stadium all-seater. Parkhead had 7,900 seats in the South Stand and 5,000 in the North Enclosure. There was standing room for 19,100 in the West Terrace and 17,800 in the East Terrace. The total capacity was 49,800 but it had been needed only for Old Firm matches. The most recent two home games against Rangers had attracted gates of 48,000. For their two European matches that season UEFA had imposed attendance restrictions.

There were two options to meet the 1 August deadline. The first was to stay at Parkhead and do no more than satisfy the requirements of *The Taylor Report* and concerns of Strathclyde Regional Council about safety. This meant spending £2.5 million to put seats on the two terraces which would give a total capacity of 34,900. The second option was to redevelop Parkhead into a modern stadium and install temporary seating in the meantime. This would cost £1.5 million.

Tom Grant said that if work started immediately the season ended, either option could be completed by September. He also reckoned that the second option could be adapted so that a full redevelopment of the stadium could be phased in and enough capacity maintained throughout the work to accommodate an average home crowd.

A month after the takeover at Parkhead notice was given of another EGM seeking to increase the share capital. But this requisition came from the new board. The meeting, on 29 April 1994, was intended to raise up to £21 million to reduce the debt, rebuild Parkhead and have money left to spend on players.

Shareholders were to be given the right they were denied earlier, to buy new shares. They would be offered 23 new ordinary shares at £1 each and 12 Preference shares for £60 each for every two shares they already held. No dividend was likely on the ordinary shares for at least three years but the Preference would produce a six per cent dividend after three years. To help shareholders take up the offer, Bank of Scotland loans were to be made available.

McCann undertook to buy up to 135,100 new ordinary shares and 5,550 new Preference shares, costing him £8.5 million altogether. If the share issue failed to raise £21 million, Celtic would either become a public limited company or form a holding company which would be public so that £5.4 million worth of shares could be offered to supporters. And another £2.5 million worth of Preference shares would be offered to a bank or financial institution.

He moved quickly to tackle the debt. McCann brought the bank borrowing facility down to £2.5 million, saving the club 0.5 per cent on the interest rate. And he made a £5 million fluctuating loan to the club at a saving of 1.25 per cent on the interest rate. If all £7.5 million of these borrowing facilities were being used, it would save the club £75,000 a year in interest charges.

The rest of the package was the same as the one offered at the November EGM. McCann's shareholding would not go above 50 per cent; if it did so as a result of the share issue, it would be brought down to 50 per cent as soon as possible. He would hold his stake until the end of December 1999 and after that no individual, family or group would hold more than ten per cent.

He would introduce one share, one vote, instead of the current ten shares, one vote. And, as promised before the takeover, he almost completely removed the right of directors to refuse to transfer shares. The right had been used ruthlessly by the previous board in an attempt to keep control of the club. From now on there would be only a few technical grounds on which the board would not transfer shares. The new régime would play by new rules.

II

PART OF McCann's legacy was a board of which two-thirds had presided over the most disastrous period in the 106 years of Celtic Football Club. Tom Grant had the best plea in mitigation. He had tried hard by his own lights, first to fight the Kelly-White axis, then to sow peace and finally to act as go-between. As the stadium director his whole livelihood had been at risk. But he had been offered advice and even financial protection by Low and Keane and he had still allowed himself to be sucked into a pernicious voting pact.

Jimmy Farrell had proved himself to be an outspoken fighter when his seat on the board was threatened, but he had been a long time getting to the barricades. At times McGinn appeared to show more interest in his role with the SFA and even when an emergency board meeting was called at two hours' notice to strip White and Smith of their executive powers he was anxious to get away to Zürich.

Finally Kevin Kelly, chosen to be the fall-guy chairman of the club, jumped into the role with both feet first. Over-anxious to avoid conflict, willing to skirt around issues instead of confronting them, he frequently appeared unaware of the true situation in spite of being Chairman. He was pushed out in front of the cameras to act as master of ceremonies to David Smith at the infamous last Press conference about Cambuslang.

At the very last, Grant and Kelly found the courage to turn down a substantial sum of money for the sake of Celtic, and they deserve credit for that. But none of the directors McCann inherited would find a place on the board of any well-run modern company. The best they could hope for was an eventual honourable discharge from their responsibilities.

What, though, of the future? McCann was committed to reducing the maximum holding in the club to ten per cent from 1 January in the year 2000. When the legal side of the takeover was completed, the departing directors had been able to commit themselves and their immediate families. Some of their supporters sold their shares to Gerald Weisfeld.

He had increased his stake after the takeover from 18 per cent to 25.6 per cent. If the new constitution were implemented his excess holding would have to be reduced if the stake had not already been diluted through the new share issue. And the new rules would prevent a concerted grouping from taking control. There was to be no chance of a Weisfeld grandson joining with a future directors gradnsons joining to form a new dynasty. The days of the dynasty were to be finished for ever.

Lou Macari was still the man on the field. He was to have a chance to show what he could do when there was money in the kitty for players. He had been a popular choice with the fans and he understood Celtic and its traditions from the inside. He would not be indulged if he did not produce results but he was to be given a chance to deliver.

One of McCann's ambitions is to have a single Celtic supporters' organisation and he has told Celts For Change that he would like them to be part of it. 'We have hundreds of letters saying we represent the support,' said Matt McGlone. 'We have had meetings with Fergus McCann and representatives of other groups. He wants one united organisation.'

Before that can happen, however, there is some bridge building to be done. The official supporters organisations had 'treated us with contempt,' said Sweeney.

Celts For Change set a precedent. Other fans have held protests and even short-lived boycotts for or against the firing of managers. West Ham fans forced amendments to proposals for a controversial Bond scheme. But none have waged such a sustained and well-organised campaign. They spent time gathering support before taking action. Their actions never went too far ahead of their support. Within weeks of the takeover a group of fans of another Scottish club, Falkirk, were beginning to employ similar tactics. It is hard work and by the end of the campaign all the Celts For Change committee said 'Never again,' although gradually each admitted that if the club ever hit the same depths he just might do something similar.

It took a thriller writer, Gavin Lyall, to sum up democracy in 14 words when one of his heroes said: 'Democracy is enough people standing up and saying: "You can't bloody well do that." '

In the last century governments felt ordinary men and women needed neither education nor the vote; they would only be confused by political issues. Today there are company directors who feel the same way: ordinary men and women do not have to understand business even though it controls their lives: what they wear, eat and read, and whether they even work at all. The Celtic story proves them wrong. Any punter who can appreciate fine play and calculate the points for his pools can understand business if he is not fobbed off with jargon. And that is the best defence against the misuse of business. Old family cliques and secret deals are no protection.

Most Scottish and English football clubs are, legally, companies and have to be run as such. But their long-term strength lies in the loyalty of their supporters. The clubs have to return that loyalty. Whether the cry is 'You can't bloody well do that' or 'Sack the board', the punter has a right to his say. As Brendan Sweeney of Celts for Change said: 'We have shown fans all over the world what can be done.'

Chapter Sixteen

THE LAST MYSTERY UNCOVERED

BUT THE story was still not over . . .

That first week after the takeover had been chaotic, with accountants combing through the files trying to get to the bottom of things. It added to the strains in the relationship between Dempsey and McCann. The euphoria of victory and the media spotlight that went with it quickly subsided in the practical demands of business and to Dempsey it seemed as if Parkhead was full of non-Celtic people. But these people were essential to drawing up a thorough financial review of what they had taken over. It was quite possible the rebels had bought themselves a pig in a poke. McCann offered Dempsey a seat on the board but the offer was turned down.

At the end of that first week there was a party at Celtic Park to celebrate the takeover but the atmosphere was more like a wake. Dempsey did not attend. Many of the guests went on to another party at Jimmy Farrell's house. All the directors were there, as were their wives. Kevin Kelly played the piano and sang Irish songs at the top of his voice. It was a little bizarre: after the long, stressful battles, the changing alliances among the old board, the fierce opposition some of the directors had shown to the new members of the board, suddenly they were all supposed to be the best of pals.

Dempsey announced he would be leaving the country to spend five of the next 12 months in the States. He went to Grand Cayman and then on to the USA. On 7 April the new board were to requisition the EGM to recapitalise the club. Although the resolutions for the EGM followed closely the proposals put forward at the EGM nearly six months earlier in November, and supported by Weisfeld, nothing could be taken for granted. Weisfeld had to be on McCann's side for the plan to succed.

Nothing had been said explicitly to arouse fears that Weisfeld would not support McCann but he had continued buying shares after the takeover, paying between £275 and £300 each, and the EGM's resolutions would have the effect of diluting his shareholding. Low opened negotiations with him. But this time there would be no media circus as there was when Smith was negotiating with the Haughey-Weisfeld consortium.

Low's first step was to meet Willie Haughey at Parkhead on 21 March. That meeting began to clear up the mystery of Haughey's and Weisfeld's behaviour. Until then Low's meetings with Haughey had been simply to learn what he and Weisfeld intended to do in the urgent build-up to the takeover. Now they had a chance to exchange more information. Haughey had believed that Dempsey had been supporting his plan to buy out the pact members and he had pursued the plan believing it was the only way to remove them.

It became clear that the two flanks of the rebel forces might have been willing to withdraw at the same time. That would have left the old board with no chance of being bailed out financially. The McCann and Weisfeld groups could have saved each other around £1 million.

Right up until 1.30 a.m. on the morning of the takeover, David Smith had been holding out the promise of a deal to Haughey. Once the takeover had taken place, Weisfeld had continued buying shares in order to try to protect the investment he had already made.

Haughey approaches everything he does with the same bouncing enthusiasm. He had originally bought shares simply to attend the November EGM, to 'see history being made', as he put it, believing that the rebels would win the day. When he got there and listened to what he called 'the self-preservation society' on the board defending their position, he had jumped up and offered to buy Michael Kelly's shares for £350. It was Weisfeld who, tugging at Haughey's sleeve, told him to make the offer to all the directors.

Low took Willie upstairs to meet Fergus. The outcome was a meeting between Low and Weisfeld at Celtic Park a week later. In the meantime the fans had shown their support of the new régime by returning in droves. The first home game after the takeover, against Motherwell, attracted a crowd of 36,000. Jim Doherty flew over from Toronto for the weekend. The atmosphere was ecstatic. Only the final result was disappointing.

Weisfeld had his meeting at Celtic Park on 29 March. He and Low got on well but it was clear they must reach agreement. Low was pleased that Weisfeld appointed Jack Gardiner of the law firm Bird Semple as his adviser. Gardiner was shrewd and knowledgeable and when the two men met for the first time on 1 April, the real Good Friday, they found they talked the same language.

Brian Dempsey had returned from America and was keen to meet Weisfeld again. At the 23 April Celtic v Kilmarnock match, he arranged to be at the same table but Weisfeld did not show up that day. Haughey was there though and spoke his mind to Dempsey, whom he blamed for misleading him during his attempt to buy out the pact members.

Weisfeld now held 26 per cent of the shares yet he was not represented on the board. He had supported McCann in the past but that was no guarantee he always would. Although he might have found it hard to explain any blocking action at the EGM to the fans and to other shareholders, he might have felt justified in preventing his expensively acquired shareholding from being diluted. An agreement with Weisfeld was important.

If the EGM resolutions failed the board would have to consider Plan B, which was to put Celtic into receivership. It was McCann's money which had stopped the receivers being called in. He had taken over from the bank as the club's biggest creditor. All he had to do was to call in his loan. Once the receivers were in, he could have bid for the club and bought it from the receivers.

A ruthless businessman would have made this Plan A. It would have saved him money and hassle. Creditors would have been paid only a percentage, if anything, of the money owed to them by Celtic. Stoke City would have lost most of the money still owed in compensation for losing Lou Macari and his backroom staff. If Terry Cassidy won his court case, his claim for damages might have gone unpaid. The departed pact members would have received nothing for their shares.

But this was more than a company in the East End of Glasgow. This was Celtic. Receivership would have meant a break in more than a century of tradition. There are still some things which cannot be measured in money.

Plan B had to remain as a threat and in the final days before the EGM, which everyone prayed would be the last EGM, that threat was in the air. On Monday, 25 April, Weisfeld's team met at the Moat House Hotel beside the Scottish Exhibition and Conference Centre on the Clyde. Weisfeld himself was in Beverly Hills but a telephone conferencing link was set up. They drew up their requirements for supporting the proposals.

McCann's team met the next morning. That afternoon both sides met at the offices of law firm Semple Fraser Haniford di Ciacca in St Vincent Street, a block away from the Bank of Scotland. With Low were the firm's managing partner David Semple and Derek Ellery. Facing them were Jack Gardiner and George Boyle, his assistant from Bird Semple, along with Haughey, Michael McDonald and Paul Waterson.

That meeing went on for the next 26 hours.

Gardiner had done everything right for the Weisfeld team. He had arranged all his proxy votes for the meeting, and his powers of attorney and had lodged caveats in both Glasgow and Hamilton Sheriff Courts in case of any attempt to take legal action against them before the EGM. Low realised Gardiner had probably countered the receivership option. That threat could now be used only if the EGM rejected McCann's proposals. If he had been on the other side of the table, Low would have advised Weisfeld to call their own EGM and offer to take over McCann's loan to the club.

Fatigue frayed the tempers of the negotiators with Low at one point threatening, 'It's fucking war.' But the difference between the two sides came down to the level of underwriting they would commit themselves to for the share issue. Eventually they reached agreement. Low went home for an hour's nap before the Celtic v St Johnstone game. Instead, he woke up 13 hours later.

On 29 April 1994 the first Celtic shareholders meeting for four years had no split. The voting was 90-nil for the proposals. It was all over in little more than an hour. 'A rather boring meeting, I'm afraid,' McCann told reporters. 'No fights.'

The £21 million share issue was approved and the meeting was told the rebuilding of Celtic Park would begin that summer. Over the next two years £24 million would be spent on helping Paradise live up a little more closely to its name. The club at last had a new future. The Celtic story is still not over . . . but this one is.